Advance praise for Golden Stripes

Captain Parani writes with clarity and authority. Through a blend of anecdotes and analyses, this book motivates the mariner to lead effectively at sea.
Captain Steve Clinch, Chief Inspector of Marine Accidents, Marine Accident Investigation Branch, UK

I believe Captain Parani's book addresses a gap in maritime education and one that maritime universities are starting to realize. For too long we have focused on increasing the technical competencies of our graduates and are now realizing the most important ship in their career will be leader'ship'. Golden Stripes highlights the value of leadership through stories, quotes and experience and is an excellent primer for cadets and a companion book for experienced mariners.
Glenn Blackwood, Chairman, International Association of Maritime Universities; Executive Board, World Maritime University, Sweden; Executive Director, Memorial University of Newfoundland, Canada

As President of the Nautical Institute I believe leadership and human factors will be two of the most important issues in our industry in the coming decade. Golden Stripes comprehensively addresses these issues and provides an easily understandable template for ships' officers to develop a personal code of ethics and standards for their careers.
Captain Robert McCabe, FNI, MSc Mgmt. President, Nautical Institute, London

In Golden Stripes Captain Parani combines the credibility of his seafaring experience with his talent as a master storyteller to reveal the leadership challenges at sea and his strategies for staying on course. He transports you to the heart of the action in the engine room, the deck, and the bridge of the ship. Long after you've put this book down, you'll remember the hard-earned and valuable leadership lessons Captain Parani so artfully conveys. It's a one-of-a-kind book that every mariner will treasure.
James M Kouzes, co-author of the bestselling The Leadership Challenge; Dean's Executive Fellow of Leadership, Leavey School of Business, Santa Clara University, USA

This is a very interesting book on leadership that draws on the author's maritime experience. It is both entertaining and informative, and provides practical advice for those who aspire to a management or leadership role.
Professor Jane Smallman, PhD, CSci, CMarSci, FIMarEST, President Institute of Marine Engineering, Science & Technology, London

Captain Parani has keenly observed and noted what he has learnt in his career. There is a coherence and an elegance to what he offers his colleagues in this book. I am convinced that Captain Parani has more to say, more to offer, more to explain and elaborate, but he has the good sense of knowing where to stop and the dignity of telling us what we need to know.

Professor Sidney Dekker, MA MSc PhD, School of Humanities, Languages and Social Sciences, Griffith University, Australia; best-selling author on human factors and safety
www.sidneydekker.com

Finally a book on leadership at sea that is anchored in real life where the consequences of leadership failure are deadly. This book lays out clearly with numerous dramatic stories how leadership, team work, training, and safety management all have to combine to make this major industry work for all of us. What we learn applies to all of our daily endeavours.

Edgar H Schein, PhD, Professor Emeritus, MIT Sloan School of Management, Massachusetts; author of *Organizational Culture and Leadership*

What does it mean to be a leader on board merchant ships and what does it take to become a good and effective leader in the merchant navy? These are the two most prominent questions Captain Parani provides answers to with his excellent book on leadership in the merchant navy. Based on his own experience Captain Parani gives evidence of how important proper and effective leadership is for the safe conduct of the ship and at the same time explains how the necessary skills can be acquired by future but also present shipmasters.

Captain Willi Wittig, MSc, Associated Professor of Maritime Human Resource Management, HSB - City University of Applied Sciences, Bremen; Deputy President, The International Federation of Shipmasters' Associations (IFSMA), London

Golden Stripes describes a particularly powerful and effective approach to developing leadership skills on a ship – or anywhere else. Captain Parani weaves together lessons learned from his own remarkable career with cutting-edge insights from psychological research on expertise to produce this invaluable step-by-step guide to becoming a leader on the high seas.

Robert Pool, PhD, co-author of *Peak: Secrets from the New Science of Expertise*

There are numerous books on leadership, but few have been more concisely written as Golden Stripes. *Focused on the merchant mariner, it contains material that is applicable to all persons in leadership positions and to those who aspire to become effective leaders. I wish it had been available when I first became an officer.*

Captain Dennis L Bryant, US Coast Guard (ret); Principal, Bryant's Maritime Consulting

This is an extraordinary book, from a real captain of the seas. Leadership is usually a mushy subject, but I was gripped by this. Highly recommended for anyone who wants to lead anything, anywhere.

Richard Koch, author of million-copy-selling *The 80/20 Principle*

Effective leadership combines natural ability with learnt skills, learnt mostly through experience and reflection. Captain Parani shares with us a wealth of his own observations and experiences, and also draws on those of others. He brings vividly to life what it means to be a great leader of mariners, whether in port or in the loneliness of the high seas.

Andrew Mayo, Professor of Human Capital, Middlesex University Business School, UK; Founder of Mayo Learning International and author of *The Human Value of the Enterprise*

Leadership at sea is an important issue worldwide. The Dutch Shipmasters Association (NVKK), of which I am a member, has identified it as one of its priorities. Leadership is a complex, multi-faceted issue inspiring considerable theoretical studies. Captain Parani has brought maritime leadership down to earth, or rather sea level: practical, encouraging us to never stop thinking, to never stop asking, to never stop learning. These are the most important traits for us all.

Captain Ed Verbeek, Verbeek Nautical Consultancy and Training, Netherlands

Golden Stripes *has the potential to become a standard exposé on leadership for the maritime industry. Captain Parani uses a very balanced mix of known industry cases, anecdotes from his own experience as well as leadership concepts and pragmatic advice. Any experienced mariner will be reminded of countless situations in the past, where the book's content should have been applied. Any cadet can use it as a source of what to expect and how to drive their own progress in leadership. But over and above many of the concepts promoted by* Golden Stripes *can be easily transferred to other demanding industries, where being a responsible leader can save lives or otherwise prevent huge damages. Captain Parani, thank you for writing this book!*

Markus Schmitz, Executive Committee Member, InterManager; Managing Director, SOFTimpact Ltd., Cyprus

This book is a must read! Great leaders produce great results. Each one of us is a leader! Whether leading as the Captain of vessel, a CEO, a stay-at-home parent, a teacher, a coach or as someone leading their own lives. The ideas that you will get from this book, based on years of experience at sea, will inspire, stimulate, encourage and teach you the things that great leaders do. Congratulations Captain Parani on a wonderful book.

Steven R Shallenberger, author of *Becoming Your Best, the 12 Principles of Highly Successful Leaders;* founder of Becoming Your Best Global Leadership, USA

Golden Stripes *is a great leadership handbook, that has lessons not just for mariners but also for professionals from all walks of life.*

John Adair, author of the best-selling series which include *Effective Leadership, Effective Communication* and *Effective Teambuilding*

Golden Stripes *makes an important contribution to seafarers of all stripes desiring to become better leaders. It does a terrific job of blending leadership theory with practical, hands-on maritime experience. Captain Parani has clearly caught the vision of the transformative power of being a professional – something near and dear to my heart.*

Bill Wiersma, Principal of Wiersma and Associates USA; bestselling author of *The Power of Professionalism – The Seven Mind-Sets That Drive Performance and Build Trust*

This book is a must read for anyone who manages risks and wants to lead safely. Golden Stripes *shares lessons learned from real-life cases and potential solutions for such situations.*

James Roughton, CSP, CRSP, CET, R-CHMM, Six Sigma Black Belt; author *Safety Culture: An Innovative Leadership Approach* and *Job Hazard Analysis, Second Edition: A Guide for Voluntary Compliance and Beyond* and of the training course, 'Why is it Important to Understand the Perception of Safety?' www.safetycultureacademy.com

Golden Stripes *applies Captain Parani's experience, wisdom and learning to leadership and team working at sea. His deep knowledge is communicated in a beautifully readable and engaging book, sharing lessons that will change your thinking about the importance of team working and leadership at sea. It is a delight to read and the stories Captain Parani tells bring the vital lessons to life for any seafarer.* Golden Stripes *is indeed a rich treasure trove of knowledge about leadership and team working at sea.*

Professor Michael West, Professor of Organizational Psychology, Lancaster University Management School, UK; author of *Effective Teamwork: Practical Lessons from Organizational Research*

Golden Stripes *has leadership lessons from the sea which are helpful for all professionals. I used some of the practical techniques in my hospital and it made my life easier.*

Dr Rajesh Botchu, MBBS, MS(orth), MRCSI, MRCSEd, FRCR, Consultant Musculoskeletal Radiologist, The Royal Orthopaedic Hospital, Birmingham, UK

Golden Stripes *makes an important contribution to leadership at sea. By asking seafarers to focus on safety management and more importantly safety leadership Captain VS Parani ensures safety is and should be the primary concern for those charged with the safety of* others.

Robert B Hafey, RBH Consulting USA; author of *Lean Safety: Transforming your Safety Culture with Lean Management*

Golden Stripes *is a well-researched and valuable book for all commanders, both in shipping and in aviation.*

Martin Leeuwis, Fighter Pilot & Airline Pilot KLM (retd.), and publisher of over 30 aviation humour and cartoon books, www.humor.aero

With this book, Captain Parani sails through a sea of leadership stories and offers us a vista of inspiring examples and experiences. Skip this book at your own peril!

Jurgen Appelo, Top 50 Leadership Expert on *Inc.*;
author *of Managing for Happiness*

When I wrote my books on decision making and meeting technique, I was thinking about life on dry land. VS Parani's remarkable book Golden Stripes *takes management into a different dimension and environment. 71% of the earth's surface is water, and we should all take lessons from shipping more seriously. I am humbled and delighted that Captain Parani found some of my ideas useful in the context of leadership at sea.*

David Wethey, author of *DECIDE: Better Ways of Making Better Decisions*
and *MOTE: The Super Meeting*

Golden Stripes *is a valuable and accessible handbook on leadership for seafarers. Captain Parani is a lively and engaging storyteller who draws together true and compelling maritime examples of best practice and disasters to illustrate the many lessons of leadership in a very practical manner.*

Dr Jacquie Drake, Founder and CEO, www.cool-leadership.com

Is a leader born or made? Whatever you believe it is commonly accepted, that leadership qualities can improve through study, training, methodical application and practice, continuous improvement makes the difference between a good leader and a great leader. Robust leadership is particularly important at sea, where mistakes or omissions are judged harshly. This book is a very useful tool for those who strive to effectively lead their teams at sea, but also very relevant to those who communicate with vessel Masters, giving a strong insight to challenges associated with command, effectively breaching the divide between shore and ship. In addition to merchant seafarers, I see it equally useful to ship owners, ship managers, operators, charterers, port agents and port managers.

Michael Taliotis, International Chairman,
The Institute of Chartered Shipbrokers, London

Golden Stripes *is essential reading for all those at sea. Captain Parani covers both the soft skills and hard knowledge required to lead at all levels. He shows us a maritime frame of mind that allows for the many uncertainties in the maritime environment, and does so with depth (from many safety investigations), with breadth (using insights from Ayn Rand to Napoleon), and with clarity. I highly recommend this book.*

Andrew St George, author of *Royal Navy Way of Leadership*; founding partner
Fathomicity Ltd., UK

GOLDEN STRIPES

GOLDEN STRIPES

LEADERSHIP ON THE HIGH SEAS

Captain VS Parani,
FNI, FICS, MIMarEST

Whittles Publishing

Published by
Whittles Publishing Ltd.,
Dunbeath,
Caithness, KW6 6EG,
Scotland, UK

www.whittlespublishing.com

© 2017 Seawise Ltd.

Reprinted 2018

ISBN 978-184995-314-6

Disclaimers

*The views expressed in this book are the author's own and
do not necessarily represent the views of his employers and
organizations he is associated with. Names have been altered
where necessary to respect the privacy of the characters.*

*This book is for both men and women, though the author has used
male nouns and pronouns extensively for ease of reading.*

*The case studies in this book are meant only to support a point
being made and are not meant to blame anyone or comment
adversely on any individual or organisation.*

To All The Brave Mariners At Sea

CONTENTS

Note to reader: all the black and white text illustrations are repeated in full colour in a separate section.

INTRODUCTION

A GLIMPSE FROM THE GANGWAY

We all came from the sea. And it is an interesting biological fact that all of us have in our veins the exact same percentage of salt in our blood that exists in the ocean, and, therefore, we have salt in our blood, in our sweat, in our tears. We are tied to the ocean. And when we go back to the sea – whether it is to sail or to watch it – we are going back from whence we came.

– John F Kennedy, 35th US president.

He was also a lieutenant in the US Navy, where he received the Navy and Marine Corps medal for brave leadership at sea

IT WAS THE MID-1990s. I was a newly promoted third officer. Having just passed my navigator's qualifying exams, I was sure that I could sail smoothly through my career in shipping.

Little did I know that my confidence would be shaken, and my leadership questioned, on my very first day!

The second engineer and I stepped up the gangway to board a 70,000-tonne crude oil tanker. We were the relief crew. The seamen on board were happy to see us; our arrival meant some of them would soon be meeting their families. For others, who were staying on board, we carried letters from their families (no internet in those days).

The ship towered over the pier, and it was a real beauty with its fine lines and well maintained paintwork. The humming of the generators and the cargo pumps working at full capacity filled my ears. I didn't know it then, but this would soon serve as the background score for an action-packed day.

We went up the gangway and were directed to the captain's office. With greying hair and towering stature, the captain reassuringly looked the part of an experienced mariner. Calm and composed, he welcomed us to the ship. After introductions, I enthusiastically changed into my overalls to familiarise myself with the ship.

Later that evening, we completed cargo operations and were ready to sail. We were at an oil terminal in a river, and it would take us a few hours to reach the sea. There were four others on the wheelhouse; the captain, the chief officer, an able seaman and the harbour pilot. The chief officer would monitor the ship's position, while also helping me familiarise myself with the navigation equipment, and the able seaman (AB) was at the steering, while the captain and pilot focused on manoeuvring the ship.

The orange glow of the setting sun provided a serene backdrop for the manoeuvre. Once the ropes were cast off and we had cleared the berth, we increased speed to around 14 knots to counter the strong opposing current. For a while, things seemed to be going as planned. Apparently feeling well in control, the captain asked the chief officer to go to the ship's office to check some calculations.

Suddenly, chaos.

The ship started swinging rapidly to starboard and turned towards the rocks. Alarms, buzzers, and flashing lights were set off everywhere on the bridge. The fault alarm on the steering system flashed red. We had lost control of the rudder, and our ship was hurtling towards the rocks at 70,000 tonnes per metre per second.

The chief engineer called from the engine room to confirm that we had indeed lost our steering. Recalling the emergency procedure, I switched over to the back-up system. Nothing. I had no idea what to do next; I had joined just hours before. I looked out, and all I could see was the cliff getting closer and bigger.

'What the hell is going on?' I turned around to see our captain standing behind me.

'Nothing's working!'

His eyes widened, and for a moment, I knew he could read my helplessness. I expected him to act immediately. Instead, he seemed to be running around in circles for what seemed like an eternity. To make matters worse, the chief officer, a few decks below, was probably unaware of our imminent danger. As the seconds ticked by, bringing us closer and closer to disaster, it was clear that the captain was not going to save the day.

Finally, the harbour pilot rushed in, looking as if he was going to explode. I quickly told him that the steering had failed and his anger subsided. He took a deep breath and straightened his posture. His order resounded clearly through the bridge: 'Reverse engines and drop both anchors.'

The bridge, the engine room, and anchor stations briefly buzzed with activity. And then the ship shuddered, as its engines strenuously moved astern to break the ship's enormous momentum. The anchors emerged from the chain locker and held onto the riverbed, and a huge dust cloud fell over the forecastle. We had finally stopped, less than 100 metres from the rocky cliff.

Once the ship had settled into a safe anchored position, the pilot took control again, and calmly said, 'Let's fix the rudder and move on.'

And then he lit a cigarette.

I looked around and glanced at the crew who, like me, were still nervous wrecks. The captain, ragged and sweaty, took a few minutes to regain his composure. He had frozen at a critical moment, and so had I. The harbour pilot, on the other hand, had saved our ship, and our lives, and had prevented an oil spill into the river. His ability to take quick decisions had singled him out as the leader, and the golden stripes on his uniform seemed to shine brighter than ours.

This event helped shape the rest of my sea career. I made a vow in that moment to never again be unprepared in an emergency. I would not freeze at a critical moment. My ship, my machinery, and my crew would be ready for anything.

There was just one problem. How was I going to get there? What were the skills I lacked, and how could I acquire them?

EARNING MY STRIPES

I seem to have been only like a boy playing on the seashore, and diverting myself in now and then finding a smoother pebble or a prettier shell than ordinary, whilst the great ocean of truth lay all undiscovered before me.

– Isaac Newton, physicist and mathematician

It would take me another 12 years at sea before I began seeing some answers. By then, I had gone through several more crises and high-pressure situations. I had sailed in stormy weather, loaded the ship to its marks, brought a ship into port with damaged machinery, carried out critical repairs, energised a demoralised crew, and handled difficult visitors – including pirates – to the ship. Those years in shipping taught me many lessons and were pivotal in shaping my character and honing my seamanship skills.

This period also brought its share of variety. I worked on old-fashioned general cargo ships, modern container ships, crude oil tankers, and anything from simple bulk carriers to highly automated self-unloaders. We carried all kinds of cargo, worked with different machinery and called at ports in almost all continents. As I worked with professionals from different nations, I soon realised we shared similar strengths and weaknesses.

Not long after, I realised my childhood dream. Growing up in the backdrop of the Port Blair naval base in the Bay of Bengal, I had always wanted to be a ship's captain. The sense of independence at sea, the opportunity to see new places, the appeal of wearing a uniform, the prospect of doing hands-on work, and the ability to start earning a decent salary while still in my teens, made this my only career option.

I worked hard. I learnt from salty mariners. I memorised manuals on ship-handling and technical operations. At 29, I became one of the youngest captains in a fleet of over 200 ships of the Mediterranean Shipping Company, one of the largest shipping companies in the world. This was a great honour, though it also meant I had to hone my seamanship skills further, and fast.

I loved the feel of the ship moving with the rhythm of the sea. I thoroughly enjoyed working with a gritty team of seafarers. I had realised my childhood dream.

I had also built a reputation for solving challenges, or at least that's what my bosses told me when I was given tough assignments. Moreover, since I loved the shipping industry, I spent my vacations as a trainer in a local maritime academy, and as an assistant mooring master at an offshore oil terminal.

One day, during my holidays, the director of our corporate office called me in for a chat.

'I like your enthusiasm,' he said. 'How would you like to head the Safety and Quality Department in our Hong Kong office?'

This was an opportunity most could only dream of. Instead of managing one ship, I would be in charge of the entire fleet. It meant my team would handle unique situations on a daily basis. It also meant several sleepless nights supporting ships in need. Then again, the added responsibilities and challenges meant greater fulfilment.

Ever the adventurer, I happily said yes.

As I began to deal with issues from a larger perspective, I gained insights into the root cause of many problems and how they can be prevented. Every day, I was required to take several decisions that included balancing profitability and ship safety, and so I started to learn what worked best on ships and for the company. I also helped improve and develop new processes.

But even then, why in a fleet using the same set of procedures, were ships performing differently?

Six years later, I got more answers; this time from a different perspective. I was now responsible for our Crewing and Training Department in Cyprus. I used my skills to coach my seafaring colleagues in areas where they needed advice, and helped to advance their careers. Surrounded by over 8,000 seafarers, I began to see, and even predict to some extent, which people would have greater success at work.

Throughout my career, I have had the good fortune of working alongside some very talented people. My professional association with the Nautical Institute, the Institute of Chartered Shipbrokers, and the Institute of Marine Engineering, Science and Technology, as well as my Master's studies in navigation, law, and business, connected me to many industry experts. As we compared notes, I realised there were many more who were asking the same question that I was: What makes some professionals better leaders than others?

WHY IS STRIPES ABOUT LEADERSHIP?

Everything starts and ends with leadership. Nothing else we accomplish, no other priority we pursue, is of much consequence if we do not have sound and effective leadership in place to enact it. We all have a responsibility to develop our own leadership potential and that of the Sailors.

– Admiral Michael G Mullen, US Navy

DURING MY TWO DECADES IN THE SHIPPING INDUSTRY, there have been several high profile maritime casualties: the *Estonia*, with a loss of 852 lives; the KM *Bismas Raya-2, Dashun,* and the *Sewol,* each of which reported over 300 dead. Other prominent maritime casualties of this period include the *Erika, Prestige, Rena, MOL Comfort, Svendborg Mærsk, El Faro,* and *Costa Concordia*. Almost all of these accidents cost their respective companies and insurers millions of dollars.

Incidents such as these, as well as other, earlier, events further fuelled my quest for answers. As I sifted through past investigation reports from the *Titanic, Herald of Free Enterprise, Scandinavian Star, Bow Mariner, Amoco Cadiz, Morro Castle, Mycene, Betelgeuse, Andrea Doria, Stockholm, Torrey Canyon, Sea Empress, Braer,* and the *Exxon Valdez*, it occurred to me that the *Costa Concordia* incident occurred exactly 100 years after the sinking of the *Titanic*. What were the lessons we hadn't yet learnt that we should have, ages ago?

In my research, I also considered the significant harm smaller accidents can cause. For example, crew injuries, cargo damages, oil spills, port state detentions, and machinery damages, cost lives or money, or both. Moreover, environmental pollution and commercial losses also negatively impact a shipping company's reputation.

In the end, one common feature stood out: **Every incident, on some level or the other, resulted from a failure in leadership!**

With the answer staring right at me, I began my next quest: How could I learn more about leadership at sea? To my surprise, I was unable to find a single book on leadership for merchant mariners. Every bookstore and library that I checked turned up empty. This was considerably disconcerting, particularly when you consider the following:

- Ships are expensive; a 19,000 TEU[1] new-build container ship is approximately worth 140 million US dollars, a very large crude-oil carrier (VLCC)[2] 96 million US dollars, and a Cape-size bulk-carrier[3] 53 million US dollars.

- Most passenger ships being delivered with 5,000 berths cost upwards of a billion US dollars.

- Every ship carries on it human lives and several million dollars worth of cargo; also the potential air and sea pollution, should things go wrong, is high.

- Almost every human on this planet depends on commercial ships because they carry over 90 per cent of the world's traded goods.

If you look, you'll find at least one object in every room of your home that made its journey there by ship. As global consumers, we rely heavily on ship activity to carry the goods we buy and sell. Yet there isn't one book that focuses on the importance of leadership in commercial shipping.

Mahatma Gandhi's words inspired me to 'be the change I wanted to see in the world'. So there I was. I decided to share the lessons on leadership that I had started gathering as a young officer, up until today. It was thus that *Golden Stripes* became a book on leadership on the high seas, by a mariner, for the mariner.

Leadership skills are universal. From Lao-Tzu to Peter Drucker, the philosophy of leadership has remained more or less the same over 2,000 years. But when at sea, the context in which leadership is applied is vastly different from that applied by a banker or a marketing manager. Unlike most decisions made in the boardroom, decisions and actions at sea can have immediate life or death consequences.

---

1 Twenty-foot Equivalent Unit (i.e. a twenty-foot container is one TEU) commonly describes the carrying capacity of a container ship. A 14,000 TEU ship is around 160,000-tonne deadweight.

2 A VLCC's carrying capacity is typically in the range of 250,000-tonne deadweight.

3 A Cape-size bulk carrier is typically 175,000-tonne deadweight.

The environment which the crew calls home for months is not only unique but also constantly changing. The ocean is a life-giving, yet unforgiving environment. While the space a ship occupies is limited, a drastic change in external conditions can foist on it unforeseen variables that require leadership skills to weather them with minimum impact. These variables are what make strong leadership an eminent requirement for any mariner. This is where *Golden Stripes,* a handbook for high stakes maritime leadership, can become your most trusted companion at sea.

Golden Stripes is for all seafarers, navigators and engineers alike. I like to call it a tunnel-to-funnel leadership book.

Moreover, the valuable leadership lessons from the sea can be applied in any walk of life. In that sense, *Golden Stripes* is actually for any professional who desires not just to exist, but to excel and be a shining leader.

Leadership is all about how you can make a difference at work. No matter your experience level, I hope this guide-by-your-side will inspire you to achieve more and influence others, thereby making significant changes in your career. If you want better people around you, be the ideal that you want others to achieve.

Cast off the ropes, open your mind to all the possibilities, and chart your own course. Here's to better leadership, no matter how many stripes you have!

2

LEADERSHIP LESSONS FROM THE SEA

Seamen, with their inherent sense of order, service, and discipline, should really be running the world.

– Anonymous, *Shiphandling for the Mariner*

CHARLES DARWIN SAILED around the world on HMS *Beagle* for five years. Based on his collection of samples and observations, he published *The Origin of Species*. Had his ship foundered in the Pacific, how would we have known of his theory of evolution?

Today, in the early years of the 21st century, there are over 1,500,000 seafarers and 100,000 ships worldwide. Whether it is helping in the discovery of the theory of evolution, or supporting world trade, seafarers influence the lives of most of the 7 billion people on this planet. In almost every sense of the word, seafarers are leaders.

Seafarers have huge responsibilities on their shoulders. Most ships complete their voyage without incident, proving that many hard-working, intelligent mariners demonstrate great leadership on a daily basis. At the same time, it seems like not a day goes by when you don't hear of a collision, grounding, capsizing, contact damage, crew injury, fire, cargo loss, pollution, infringement of regulations, or machinery damage. Unfortunately, in the public mind the failures on one ship eventually counteract the daily, mindful operations on another.

Because every mariner has a responsibility to the ship, their team, the sea, and himself, every mariner has leadership responsibilities in his own right. These *responsibilities* are the real *golden stripes*!

Leadership at sea is not just defined by title. On the contrary, if a mariner has to pull rank regularly to get the job done, he is not being an effective leader. Leadership is how you energise yourself and your team to ensure the ship keeps sailing safely. It is about demonstrating the highest standards of seamanship, day after day. It is about making the right critical decisions at every turn. It is the start and the end of everything you do.

WHO IS A LEADER? IS IT JUST THE UNIFORM?

Leadership is an action, not a position.

– Donald McGannon, president, Westinghouse
Broadcasting Company

Who is a leader? You are!

A leader is not just the captain, chief engineer, or a department head. Every mariner is a leader. A navigator who executes a collision-avoiding manoeuvre at two in the morning when everyone else is asleep; an engineer who, an hour before midnight, makes rounds to ensure that all the machinery needed for the ship to keep moving is working as required; an officer who supervises the entry of his men into a tank for maintenance; and one who guides his subordinate through overhauling a purifier; each one of these is a leader.

You don't need multiple stripes, or to be 'in charge', to lead. Sure, the more stripes you accumulate, the more crew report to you. But the crisp uniform you put on with pride will never make you a leader by itself. Your performance on the job, and the respect you garner from your team, are much better declarations of your level of leadership than the number of stripes you wear.

If you are at the beginning of your career, know this: only when you excel in a smaller role will you be invited to shine in a larger one. Demonstrate your leadership in your daily tasks, no matter how small or insignificant. Little by little, you'll gain the traction and attention that will push you to greater responsibilities.

Leadership is an art, a skill, a discipline, and a mindset, all of which can be learned, and improved with practice. That you are reading this book means you are interested in developing your leadership skills. *Golden Stripes* will help you tap into your experience and that of others, and build value into each of your stripes.

WHAT DOES IDEAL LEADERSHIP LOOK LIKE? THE LIGHTHOUSE

*The Captain carried them all. For him, there was no fixed
watch, no time set aside when he was free to relax and, if
he could, to sleep. He was strong, calm, uncomplaining, and
wonderfully dependable. That was the sort of captain to have.*

– Nicholas Monsarrat, *The Cruel Sea*

There are several mariners I personally know, and many more out at sea, past and present, who display the skills and mindsets of an ideal leader. Like lighthouses, they reassure, inspire and lead the way. One such legend was Ernest Shackleton.

Sir Ernest Shackleton was a master mariner in the merchant navy, and later a polar explorer. While his leadership qualities were generally well recognised, they came to the fore on a failed mission to the South Pole. In 1914, his ship, the *Endurance,* was trapped in ice and was taking on water. Without modern radios, they couldn't signal for help. But even in a crisis such as this, Shackleton kept himself and his crew of 28 alive. The crew sailed on a lifeboat through monstrous waves, trekked through the icy Antarctic emptiness, and subsisted on a limited supply of rations for 300 days until they were rescued.

Despite his strong physique, stamina, and a tough no-nonsense manner, Shackleton was gentle and nurturing. He was known for being quick to forgive frailties, and generous without expecting anything in return. He was aptly nicknamed 'a Viking with a mother's heart'.

Shackleton clearly understood the delicate balance needed for effective leadership: being strong without being rude; being kind without being weak; being bold without being a bully; being thoughtful but not lazy; being unassuming but not timid; being proud without being arrogant; and having a sense of humour without being reckless.

Other mariners perished in similar situations. Sir Henry Hudson's crew on the *Discovery* mutinied against him soon after they failed to find the Northwest Passage, a shortcut from Europe to China. Hudson's crew felt that he was playing favourites with the distribution of food and that he was insulting his officers. He had let morale on the ship suffer and appeared to be irresolute when he needed to be strong. The mutineers set Hudson and eight others adrift on a small open boat in the middle of what is now called Hudson Bay.

Shackleton was acutely aware of the consequences if he failed in leading his team when they needed him most. He called upon his leadership skills as he and his crew adapted to the changing conditions, all the while dealing with a myriad of thoughts, feelings and actions that would either help them survive, or cause their demise. In the end, by adopting the right mind-set, Shackleton's actions helped them guard their thoughts and make the right decisions that eventually resulted in their successful rescue.

THE MINDSET OF A LEADER: THE COMPASS

Mindset change is not about picking up a few pointers here and there. It's about seeing things in a new way.

– Carol S Dweck, Mindset: The New Psychology of Success

We already know that a mindset can either help or hinder your ability to lead effectively, but what are the characteristics of an effective leadership mindset? The following 11 points and examples help illustrate the fine balance every seafarer can strive to achieve.

(i) Skilled leaders lead by expertise, not by authority

As they excel in their own area of work, good leaders share their knowledge with their team, and are keen to assist others.

Ernest Shackleton devoted plenty of his spare time learning new skills in ship handling, polar navigation, and even carrying out scientific experiments.

So even if you don't consider yourself a born leader, you can change your trajectory by upgrading or learning new skills. Because leadership skills are acquired over time, every new skill you learn is an asset you can add to your arsenal. With effort and over time, your acquired skills will become your natural skills.

Shackleton did not consider himself to be brilliant. So much so that he didn't find school 'interesting'. At the age of 15, he applied for an apprenticeship with the merchant navy. While he found the initial years at sea tough, with determination and a passion for his craft, he eventually went on to become a legend.

(ii) Genuine leaders lead by example

Authentic leaders respect and reinforce the values, systems, and code of conduct required on their ship. After they abandoned the *Endurance*, Shackleton asked his men to discard all unnecessary belongings, anything that might slow them down with extra weight. In doing so, he took the lead by throwing his gold watch and a few gold coins into the snow. The crew followed suit, showing no hesitation in discarding their personal items as well.

That's genuine leadership. You can't expect others to follow your ad hoc, irregular instructions if you don't respect the basic values you ask them to adhere to. If you fail to lead by example, you fail to lead. It's as simple as that.

(iii) True leaders inspire others

Leaders on a ship direct, coordinate, and supervise the activities of their team. They are also aware that they have a responsibility to create a positive atmosphere and a sense of community on board.

Captain Gianluigi Aponte, founder and president of the Mediterranean Shipping Company, is such a leader. During a discussion on crew welfare, such as providing internet access to them, Captain Aponte invested half a day of his valuable time offering us his inputs. Typically, we managers would have handled it, but by getting involved Captain Aponte showed us that the crew's welfare was important to him. That is the mark of a true leader.

When leaders genuinely care about the people they lead, it is reflected across the organisation. They know generating positive feelings in their team's hearts is important to sustain a safe, happy, and productive work environment. A leader makes his team's work seem lighter than it actually is. It's no wonder that Captain Aponte led his company from owning one ship to operating over 400 ships in only four decades.

Leaders truly care, and that's why people care about what they say.

(iv) Effective leaders think ahead

Practical leaders know how to plan and systematically achieve their targets. They take the initiative and are proactive rather than reactive. They are constantly anticipating challenges and ways in which to tackle them.

This has been a core value of the Maersk Group, first expressed by its founder, Arnold Peter Møller, in a letter to his son Mærsk McKinney Møller: 'No loss should befall us that cannot be prevented by constant care'.

This proactive mindset, whether on the bridge of a ship or in the engine room or the corporate boardroom, helps teams succeed. They remain one step ahead of external elements and manage challenges better than other teams. This has been one of the reasons for the success of the Maersk Group, which has grown from a one-ship company in 1886 to the shipping, trade, and energy giant that it is today.

(v) Gritty leaders have a 'can-do' attitude

Leaders need physical and mental stamina as well as the conviction that the toughest of tasks can be accomplished. Why? Simple. If a leader gives up, so will everyone else. After all, who wants to follow a negative, lazy person?

In November 2013, Captain Andreas Kristensen and his crew on board the *Britannia Seaways* showed tremendous grit and perseverance when they fought a raging fire for 13 hours. The conditions were challenging; the ship had lost all power and was rolling almost 20 degrees in rough seas off the Norwegian coast. Intense flames were spreading fast, rising to 30 metres above deck. Captain Kristensen's strong leadership ensured that the fire was brought under control. The entire crew received the 2014 International Maritime Organization (IMO) Award for Exceptional Bravery at Sea.

(vi) Dynamic leaders are passionate and committed

Shipping, like many other industries, is a stressful, hard, 24/ 7 business. Without passion and commitment, one cannot succeed. Dynamic leaders have no problem getting up every day, irrespective of their own troubles, and getting to work. They do not wait to be told what to do; they take their own initiative.

Captain Iakinthi Tzanakaki won a special 'Woman of the Sea' award at the Greek Shipping Awards 2014 for her action in protecting her tanker, *Amphitrite*, and its crew, during an incident when strong winds threatened cargo discharge at an oil terminal in Beirut.

The mooring master had assured her that he had the situation under control and that the tugs would soon arrive to assist the ship. Very soon, the wind gusts picked up speed, the tanker's mooring ropes started parting and the ship was pushed towards another tanker at the terminal.

Sensing that no help would arrive in time, Captain Tzanakaki took control. From a point where the two ships were only about 20 metres apart, she expertly manoeuvred the tanker out of imminent danger, using the engines and the thrusters. Had she not taken the initiative, everyone else would have waited for the mooring master to take action, blaming him if things had gone wrong. But that is not what passionate and committed leaders do. Instead, they channel their conviction into doing what needs to be done.

(vii) Active leaders get their hands dirty when required

Involved leaders are always willing to help out with work when needed. Leaders do not ask others to do something they themselves wouldn't do. And although they demand excellence in work, they aren't hard taskmasters.

This one time, on one of my ships a generator was unable to take a full load. This meant that the ship wouldn't have sufficient power to carry the planned number of refrigerated containers. The company could lose thousands of dollars in freight on this voyage. Even the generator specialists who attended the ship in port had been unable to fix the problem. Our second engineer, Viktor, was not in the mood to give up. He declared 'I'd like to give it another try. I need volunteers to help me'.

Astonished, the chief engineer asked 'Are you sure you can do this?'

Viktor appeared determined as he replied, 'I promise I won't make it worse than before'.

Inspired, the whole crew offered to help him. It took us 30 hours of non-stop work. But it was worth it.

No one minded the lack of sleep, the oil-soaked overalls or the dirt under their fingernails when we heard the generator's full-bodied roar. It was the sound of success. We cheered for Viktor. His leadership had motivated us to persevere, to stretch beyond our comfort level, and to achieve the seemingly impossible.

Viktor is now a chief engineer working for one of the largest gas tanker companies in the world. He is assigned prestigious projects where he supervises ships undergoing construction, modification and repair.

(viii) Influential leaders communicate well

Leaders understand that every time they communicate, it is an opportunity to influence and lead. They communicate directly and decisively, all the while striving to be understanding and respectful. The point is to be intentional without being aggressive.

After taking command, Captain David Marquet of the USS *Santa Fe* found that his crew was suffering from low morale and lacked enthusiasm. Rather than initiate new ideas, they only did 'whatever they were told to do'. In his book *Turn the Ship Around*, Captain Marquet describes how he encouraged his subordinates to take charge and make decisions, thus increasing their sense of responsibility.

Captain Marquet asked for inputs from his team and implemented their suggestions. From informal conversations to briefings to memos, he used all appropriate means of communication. He encouraged his crew to clearly express their doubts and intentions. In time, the crew now felt engaged and energised, and the results showed. From having the worst retention rate in the fleet, it now had the best. *Santa Fe* began to score higher grades on inspections. Awards followed. More officers got promoted. All this was possible because of improved communication inspired by the leader.

A leader who communicates well is the kind of leader that other shipmates respect and want to sail with; after all, a leader without people is no leader all!

(ix) Successful leaders do not strive to get followers but want to build leaders!

Visionary leaders know the voyage must go on, with or without them. They prepare for the future and the unexpected by creating more leaders who can take on more responsibilities and grow in their careers.

Well-balanced leaders are secure in their position, so they don't thrive on a soaring popularity, just to increase the number of their followers. Instead, they look for ways to uplift others and carry the whole team forward. Leaders enjoy coaching, mentoring, and training others, urging others to take on more responsibility.

When pirates boarded the *Maersk Alabama* and took Captain Phillips hostage on a lifeboat, Chief Officer Shane Murphy and Chief Engineer Mike Perry rose to the occasion and led their crew to safety, without losing a single member. Captain Phillips had ensured that in his absence his team would rise to the occasion as leaders in their own way, thus becoming instrumental in safely ending the crisis.

(x) Leaders are modest

Good leaders are modest; they respect the sea, the ship, their colleagues, and their work. Such leaders are generally open and approachable, which means that they tend to be great listeners. By listening, they ensure that they don't miss any warning signs, and also gain the admiration of their team. After all, when you give respect, you gain respect as a leader.

On the other hand, a lack of humility can seriously hurt a leader and his team. During routine tank cleaning operations, the chief officer on the *Bow Mariner* ignored the safety concerns of his junior officers. A while later, an explosion sank the ship and took the lives of 20 seamen.

Leaders who aim to serve the team and the team goal ahead of themselves earn everyone's respect. Ernest Shackleton was said to have made hot coffee for his crew when they were stranded in ice, simply to lift the general morale. His humility and his ability to put himself in a position of discomfort only raised his stature in the eyes of his crew.

(xi) Bold leaders lead with courage

As a seafarer, it takes considerable fortitude and mettle to make potentially life-altering decisions day after day. You have to exercise your judgment – judgment that comes with experience and clarity of thought. And as your team relies on your decision-making process, they also expect you to express yourself in a calm yet decisive manner, even in times of crisis.

When the *Costa Concordia* ran aground off the Italian coast and when the water was flooding in, Captain Schettino abandoned his ship before all the passengers could get off. Once he was out of the ship, there was no one to coordinate the evacuation, and as a result dozens of lives were lost. He was later criticised by the accident investigators and the prosecuting court in failing in his leadership.

On the other hand, Captain Phillips of the *Maersk Alabama* showed courage and strength when his crew was threatened by Somali pirates. He bravely asked his crew to retreat to the ship's secret citadel while he engaged with the pirates. His initiative inspired the rest of the crew to fight back and regain control of the ship. His bravery is what made his leadership not only the subject of a book and a movie but also the stuff of legends.

A leader's courage is not just required in such extreme circumstances, but also in everyday decision making. He is not afraid to take bold steps, try that much longer and harder, based on the needs of his ship, more than anyone else.

These 11 points summarise what I consider to be the traits of great leaders at sea, further affirmed by the role models – captains, chief engineers, pilots and surveyors – I've been fortunate to work with.

You may never have to face the extreme dangers that Shackleton and his men did. But even on a modern ship, there is no shortage of hazards and challenges. This is why improving leadership skills is crucial to a mariner at sea. Can one really afford not to?

THE LEADER'S STRIPES

- Leadership can and should be learnt by every professional.

- Let your leadership serve others just as a lighthouse guides ships in the right direction.

- Golden Stripes mariners have a strong inner compass, balancing the 11 effective leadership traits that help keep their team safe, energised, and efficient.

- The ideal leader is a 'Viking with a mother's heart'.

3

LEAD WITH EXPERTISE: THE KEEL OF LEADERSHIP

Ships are to little purpose without skillful Sea Men.

> – Richard Hakluyt, English writer,
> in his book *Voyages*, 1589

I GROUNDED MY FIRST SHIP at the age of 16.

It was a rowboat actually, but I learnt my lesson so well that I've never had to experience that ever again.

I grew up in the faraway Andaman Islands, where the sea and ships are always in the background. The archipelago consists of 572 emerald islands and rocks, only a handful of which are inhabited. Coral reefs, pristine lagoons, lush rainforests and the odd volcano form a scenic landscape in hues of green and blue.

During my final year in high school, I took a boating trip with seven of my friends. We set off on two rowboats on a beautiful new moon Saturday afternoon. Although we had only a limited knowledge of boating, it didn't stop us from turning down the local guide's offer of help. We figured we would just get on the boats and *'take it as it comes'*.

There were no other visitors that day, so we had the expansive backwaters all to ourselves. For the first hour or so, we raced the boats against each other until we were bored. Then we spotted a creek through one of the mangrove islands. These 'islands' are actually mangroves growing over a shallow patch of the backwaters, and we could see that the narrow creek sat below the overhanging trees. It looked mysterious enough for a bunch of teenage boys in search of adventure, so off we went.

There was room for only one boat to go through at a time, and since ours was closer to the opening, we decided to go first. As we passed the entrance, we could not help but admire the beauty of nature that surrounded us.

Suddenly, our boat touched the bottom of the creek.

The water was clear, but we had been so distracted by what was around us, as well as by the other end of the creek that we hadn't noticed the muddy bottom edging closer.

First things first, we warned our friends in the other boat to retreat. Then, we started to row in the reverse direction, but the boat was fast aground. Before we knew it, the water under us was rushing out, and fast. I would learn later that tides are highest and lowest on a new moon.

We were soon sitting helplessly on bare mud. Thankfully, the boat was flat-bottomed, so it was anchored to the seabed. Meanwhile, our friends in the other boat backtracked and stayed at the entrance of the creek to offer moral support.

With only about two hours of sunlight remaining, the last thing we wanted to do was to spend the night in the middle of a mangrove jungle among wild animals and pesky insects. The alternative was to leave the boat, reach the trees on the side of the creek, and try to reach the 'island'. We could then walk across to the edge where our friends were waiting on the other boat.

I volunteered to go first; I stripped to my underwear and got down from the boat with some help. To my horror, I gradually sank deeper into the mud until it had almost reached my neck. Thankfully, before I was completely dragged in by the mud, my friends hauled me back into the boat. Now I was dirty, nearly naked, and facing a long, cold, dark night. If only there had been mobile phones back then to call for help!

After witnessing what had just happened, our friends in the other boat decided to head back to the pier and call for help. We agreed it was the best solution, so we stayed put on our boat. They returned about an hour later with the boat handler. Armed with a machete, he cut down some branches to make a walkway over the swampy island and get to us. One by one, shoes around our necks, we got off the boat and formed a human chain to help each other out. When we eventually made our way back through the mangrove-lined lagoon and to the pier, we were still in high spirits, but fully aware of our foolishness.

As life went on, my friends each carved out paths of their own. I eventually became a ship captain, commanding ships several thousand times heavier than the rowboat, but I would never forget the lessons I learnt that day:

- On a ship, there is no substitute for expertise.
- Navigating a ship without skill and preparation is foolish and dangerous.

- You can learn some things as you go along, but don't rely on luck. The price of ignorance is high, and ignorance is not an excuse.

- Leaders who demonstrate expertise will gain the trust and confidence of their team.

WHAT IS THE IDEAL OF EXPERTISE? THE MARINER

The redeeming and ideal aspect of this breadwinning is the attainment and preservation of the highest possible skill … It is made up of accumulated tradition, kept alive by individual pride, rendered exact by professional opinion, and, like the higher arts, it is spurred on and sustained by discriminating praise. That is why the attainment of proficiency, the pushing of your skill with attention to the most delicate shades of excellence, is a matter of vital concern.

– Captain Joseph Conrad,
The Mirror of the Sea

Expertise is, as Conrad says, the highest possible level of skill. It cannot be obtained with a certificate, but rather is cultivated through a long, deliberate, and passionate learning process. Much like a keel that supports and stabilises the hull of a ship, your expertise is the basis of your leadership. Whether you are a navigator, a marine engineer, an electrical engineer, a naval architect, or a ship manager, the keel of your leadership is your level of expertise.

We go to expert doctors, architects or lawyers because they perform skilled surgery, design beautiful homes, and win most legal battles. They are appreciated for their high level of knowledge. Similarly, deck and engine officers who display excellence every single day should be appreciated by their shipmates who return home safely.

An officer's technical or navigation skills are the foundation on which he can successfully implement his other management and leadership skills. So, if the third engineer can provide more technical solutions than his superior, his subordinates will eventually call on him for solutions. But if a chief officer is able to get along well with his colleagues but unable to plan cargo, he will not be an effective leader. No other leadership attribute can take the place of superior job-specific knowledge. On the other hand, if a mariner is highly skilled in his work, he can take his leadership to the next level.

You may ask how one can measure expertise on a ship. An engineer may be good at routine monitoring of machinery, but may never have performed any repairs. Can he be called an expert? Meanwhile, a navigator may perform his watches adequately in open sea, but may never know (until it is too late), how good he is at manoeuvring through confined waters. Would it be right to call him an expert?

THE KEEL OF YOUR LEADER-SHIP CAN ONLY BE BUILT WITH SOLID EXPERTISE.

A seafarer spends a lot of time in activities that are hard to measure: thinking, planning, and solving problems. Sadly, most seafarers consider their certificates of competency to be sufficient confirmation of their abilities, only realising their shortcomings after they have been humbled by a serious incident. In other words, many a time deck or engine officers do not know *what they do not know* until they are facing a crisis.

EXPOSING THE MYTH OF COMPETENCY: THE KRAKEN

The difference between a good officer and
a great one is about ten seconds.

– Rear-Admiral Arleigh Burke, US Navy

The Kraken is a sea-monster in Scandinavian mythology. It is likened to a giant octopus and is feared for its reputation of sinking ships.

While the Kraken can no longer bring down ships, lack of expertise certainly can. What is dangerous is the inability to act purposefully in a critical situation. Ten seconds could have made the difference to the fate of the *Titanic*, the *Torrey Canyon* or the *Costa Concordia*.

You may possess a competency licence or a degree, which is indeed a recognition by the owners and the flag state of your ship that you are able to carry out your job on board. This is a recognition of your professional studies and experience from time already spent at sea. You have a lot to be proud of, and rightly so; after all, shipping is a very challenging profession, and each day spent at sea is a reward in itself. You now have a diploma, your validation: what next? How do you further hone your skill from competency to expertise?

The Kraken is only a myth. So is the belief that competence and expertise are the same. Yes, that's right; competency and expertise are often mistakenly, and dangerously, substituted for one another. There are crucial differences between these two levels of performance, and every professional mariner should understand them. The Cambridge dictionary distinguishes them as follows:

Competency: an important skill that is needed to do a job
Expertise: a high level of knowledge or skill.

When we say a seafarer is competent for that rank, it means he has completed the mandatory studies as well as several other tasks over a predetermined period, thus enabling him to take up the responsibility. Basic competency, however, prepares most officers to be task-oriented rather than situation-oriented.

A 'competent' seafarer should generally be able to perform his tasks satisfactorily, provided his environment is mostly constant. This is seldom the case at sea, where mariners are exposed to extreme ranges of weather, new ports, erratic work patterns, various cargoes, changing crew, and different types of machinery. When conditions change dramatically, competency alone cannot guarantee flawless performance.

Every day, we hear about several accidents and breakdowns occurring at sea. We read that 80 per cent of these accidents are due to human error. Should we be surprised at these statistics when the industry in general relies so heavily on competency of officers alone? While competency may be sufficient to get the job done *most* of the time, it does *not* assure the high level of performance a ship deserves.

One case that intrigued me was that of the *Royal Majesty*, a modern passenger ship that ran aground on its way from Bermuda to Boston. Though there was no loss of life or pollution, the lost revenue was estimated close to 7 million US dollars. And although it was equipped with the latest integrated bridge systems, the ship had been off track for 34 hours, and finally ran aground 17 miles from its intended course line. Strangely enough, none of the officers knew of the danger until the ship had actually grounded.

Cases like these makes you wonder: Why do such accidents happen?

Were the officers competent? For sure! They held certificates of competency from a traditional maritime nation. Were they experienced? Undoubtedly. The captain on the *Royal Majesty* was a 53-year-old

EXPERTISE ENABLES YOU TO HANDLE DYNAMIC SITUATIONS BETTER THAN COMPETENCY CAN.

mariner with 32 years of experience. The 43-year-old chief officer had spent almost three years on the same ship as a navigator. The other two navigators were in their thirties, also with sufficient experience behind them. So what does that mean for us? Even if we have the right competency certificate and experience, what else is required to avoid failure and achieve success every time?

The Kraken is a myth. Competency is only a starting point. Aim for expertise.

WHY WE NEED MORE EXPERTS LIKE JAMES COOK

A better society won't just happen. Individuals with powerful problem-solving capabilities are key.

– Robert W Galvin, former CEO, Motorola Corporation

Captain James Cook (1728–1779) was an expert seaman. Under his able leadership, his team surveyed thousands of miles of previously uncharted oceans. His charting of the coastline of Newfoundland, Australia, New Zealand and Hawaii are some of his most famous accomplishments. He also discovered the method of determining a ship's longitude through celestial observations. Captain Cook may have started his career in the merchant marine, but his expertise as a mariner took human civilisation a step forward. Still remembered today for his accomplishments, the channel between the north and south islands of New Zealand as well as a crater on the moon are both named after him.

Today, there are no new lands to be revealed. What we need to discover is how to become better at what we do. We need to find our leadership abilities within us. We need more officers leading with expertise.

> WHEN LEADERS LACK EXPERTISE, NOTHING ELSE WORKS.

The focus of the shipping industry has been to enforce regulation and monitoring by class, flag, and port-state (rightly so) to improve its standards. However, the industry has already reached a near-optimal framework of regulations and enforcement mechanisms. Moving forward, instead of relying on even more regulations, it is time for the seafarer to improve his own awareness, and in doing so, elevate own industry standards.

You may ask 'Can just one man make a difference?' Just ask Captain Schettino of the *Costa Concordia* or Captain Hazelwood of the *Exxon Valdez*. As seafarers, *we* are the true drivers of change. If we devote time to improving the shipping industry, we will find ourselves making the news for our accomplishments, rather than for incidents and tragedies.

Furthermore, there are many other areas that the current inspection regime does not necessarily focus on, or is unable to fully address, such as machinery breakdowns. When I analysed dozens of machinery damages, I saw that more than 60 per cent of them occurred within a month of the equipment being overhauled on board. In one case, a ship reported 'an abnormal sound from one of the main-engine units during manoeuvring', so they stopped the ship in safer waters to examine it. A unit decarb had been carried out the previous day in port. Closer examination revealed that the distance between the piston-crown and the skirt was 12mm instead of 2mm. The O-ring between the crown and skirt was twisted, thus preventing proper fitting. A lack of expertise had led to the omission of several key procedures.

To prevent this error, the crew could have studied engine manuals and technical circulars for information on the operation and maintenance of the machinery. The power was in their hands, but they simply didn't wield it.

Cargo damages continue to occur due to officers not being fully aware of associated problems. The annual global financial impact of cargo loss is estimated to be in the range of 50 billion US dollars! Yet there is no single regulatory mechanism to control or help prevent these incidents on a global scale. If such mishaps are mostly caused by human error, then the obvious solution to minimise such errors is to train ourselves into becoming highly motivated experts.

More often than not, most ship inspectors, owners, and even mariners consider the seafarer's lack of expertise as the root cause. The Australian Maritime Safety Authority reports that over the last few years, around 63 deficiencies in ships' fire safety systems have been found annually. Although these are port state control deficiencies, we can safely suspect that our own ships are also susceptible to fire hazards. So why can't we develop our own skills to detect and rectify these deficiencies by ourselves, especially when we have spent considerably more time on the ship than the inspector? Can we not attain the same level of expertise as the surveyor who immediately sees a problem that we missed for weeks, or even months?

WHEN DOES ONE BECOME AN EXPERT? THE MOMENT OF TRUTH

I had no means of knowing that what had happened to me was a manifestation of the sixth-sense possessed by every born seaman. You can train a man in navigation, seamanship, celestial observation, and the computing of tide, current, speed, wind, and drift, and yet he will never be a sailor unless, at the moment of truth when he is forced into a corner from which there is no way out except by instant intuitive action, he unerringly makes the right move.

– Jan de Hartog, *The Captain*

The harbour pilot who saved our ship from certain grounding on my fateful first day at sea was an expert. At least, that is how I saw him. Funny thing, he never stopped to say 'I am an expert.'

The paradox is that an expert never stops gaining expertise. For him, life is a continuous learning experience. Expertise is not an inborn talent, a set of skills, a training certificate, or a degree. Expertise is a keen awareness of one's area of work. It is a goal, much like that of perfection, and in that sense it is never fully achievable. Rather, it is the process of learning, applying, and learning some more that brings you closer to expert level. Therefore, every endeavour in your career should align with gaining expertise.

You can however, spot an expert when you see him in action. It is almost as if he has a sixth sense. He detects potential areas of concern much earlier than others and is able to react and address them quickly and effectively. He makes better decisions based on a good sense of judgment, intuition, and clarity of thought. His clarity of thought comes

EXPERTISE RESULTS FROM THE EVER-HUNGRY QUEST FOR EXCELLENCE.

from deep-seated knowledge and rich experience. The expert is more resourceful when it comes to problem solving and generally has his 'eye on the ball'.

Similarly, lack of expertise also makes itself readily apparent. This was the case when the bulk-carrier *ID Integrity* suffered a blackout and was unable to restart its main engines. The ship had to seek tug assistance to avoid being grounded on the Great Barrier Reef.

The generators had been having issues for some time but the crew simply rectified the immediate symptoms without identifying the actual cause of the failures. The root cause was that prolonged running of the generators on low load had caused the cylinders and piston-rings to become glazed. This in turn led to poor sealing, carry-over of unburnt fuel, and fouling of the turbochargers.

EXPERTS ARE BETTER PROBLEM SOLVERS.

The main engine also could not be started as the fuel pump drive mechanism had failed. Over the previous months, the engine had been operated with the fuel pump roller guides in the wrong position. Additional stress had caused cracks in several reversing links and roller guides. On that day, the reversing link completely failed and the resulting debris jammed the fuel pump drive mechanism. As a consequence, the camshaft coupling slipped, and the main engine could not be restarted. An expert engineer would have followed the best engine operation and maintenance procedures, and would have been able to accurately diagnose the fault and carry out effective repairs. When experts lead, ships are less likely to get into serious trouble.

Expertise doesn't come easily. It requires years of work, replete with challenges, crises, setbacks, and successes, all of which enable us to analyse and learn from every experience.

Experts make better leaders. When your team trusts that you know what you are doing, they respect your leadership. This inspires confidence that what you are asking is very achievable. Expertise can be gained with effort and focus. If you strive to attain this level, you'll never find yourself aground like I did back in my rowboat!

LEADERSHIP BEGINS WITH EXPERTISE

- The keel of your leadership is expertise.

- Be solution-oriented rather than task-oriented.

- Competency is only the starting point. Aim for expertise.

- The essence of expertise is that everything can and must be improved.

- Expertise is a process of becoming, becoming, and becoming.

4

HOW TO BE AN EXPERT: THE STEEL OF THE KEEL

No matter how important a man at sea may
consider himself, unless he is fundamentally worthy
the sea will someday find him out.

– Felix Riesenberg, superintendent,
New York Nautical School, 1924

ONE SAILOR'S TALE goes back to an era when ships were powered by coal and steam. A certain ship in port was unable to generate enough steam to move its engines; its boiler wouldn't start.

The ship's crew tried their best over several days but nothing seemed to work. The owner called in a boiler expert, whom we shall call Ace, to figure out the problem. The crew saw a grey-haired man in overalls walk up the gangway with a small tool bag. He asked the ship's engineers a few questions, thoughtfully nodded his head, and went to the engine room. The crew wondered if this old man could get the ship moving. They followed him in.

Ace looked at the boiler and checked a few things. Humming softly to himself, he reached inside his bag and pulled out a small hammer. He gently tapped on something. Instantly, the boiler seemed to come alive.

The crew cheered as the boiler sent steam hissing through the funnel. The expert shook hands and made his way to the ship's office, where the captain, chief engineer and the ship owner were waiting to thank him. They raised a toast to him, and let him know how much money he had saved the ship. Before leaving, Ace handed his invoice to the ship owner.

'What? $10,000 just for a tap? You were here for barely an hour. I was prepared to pay you well, but this is outrageous!'

Ace took back his invoice and scribbled something on it. He then handed it back to the ship owner who looked at it, smiled, and signed the invoice. The captain and chief engineer, who were watching this exchange the whole time, were puzzled. They peered over the ship owner's shoulder to read what Ace had scribbled on his invoice.

| Tapping with the hammer | $10 |
| Knowing where to tap | $9,990 |

Experts like Ace are everywhere. They're engineers, navigators, technicians, pilots, athletes, doctors, musicians, and chefs. And they make it look easy. But expertise, as I mentioned earlier, isn't only about talent or natural skill. It takes endless hours of study, training, practice, reflection, and effort to get to the stage where you can call yourself an expert.

So how do we become experts in what we do?

I know what you are thinking. Does experience equal expertise?

EXPERIENCE = EXPERTISE?

But although all our knowledge begins with experience,
it does not follow that it arises from experience.

– Immanuel Kant, German philosopher

Experience is a great teacher, but a person needs many more teachers to learn all that he needs to know.

Recognising the value of experience, several companies require a candidate to have spent a few years in that position before hiring that person. This makes perfect sense, because experience is indeed valuable. However, there is much more to expertise than just the number of years spent at sea.

Sometimes I have sat in a room full of navigators with a combined sea time of over 200 years, only to realise that many of them have not guided their ship through ice or anchored in an emergency. While we cannot control the types of experience we gain at sea, how can we prepare for such situations?

Research indicates that though an average person requires about 10,000 hours in a particular line of work to reach expert level, there is also evidence that time spent on the job in excess of two years does *not* mean a corresponding increase in expertise. Therefore, experience *alone* is not sufficient, and neither is it a reliable indicator of future performance.

When new regulations forced ships to use gas oil in the main engines instead of residual fuel oil, the industry saw several ships suffer from blackouts and engine damage. Which begs the question:

Even with experienced mariners operating these ships, why did such incidents still occur? Experts need to perform even when pushed outside their comfort zone, but is 'propulsion hours' a sufficient guarantee for high performance?

Practice makes perfect; our repeated tasks in navigation, cargo work or machinery operation makes us better in our jobs, but is our method of work the *best* practice? Sea time alone is inadequate to make a claim of having acquired expertise. Only a commitment to *deliberate, curious, analytical,* and *structured learning* can lead to a level of expertise that will boost your leadership.

SEA TIME: WHEN JUST EXPERIENCE IS NOT ENOUGH

Many officers spend much time in perfecting themselves in deep sea navigation, where the ship is not endangered, but make no effort to acquaint themselves with conditions such as tides, currents, etc., when coming into port, because the Captain or Pilot will then be taking responsibility. This is where the real danger exists.

– Merchant Marine Officer's Handbook

There are over 200 groundings and contact damages in harbours every year, each costing half a million dollars on average, and this has remained constant even as we make rapid technological advances in the 21st century.

Usually, bridge teams navigate the ship until just outside the port, and then the pilot takes over the manoeuvre. Inadequate preparation by the ship's navigators means they rely too heavily on the pilot, increasing the possibility of human error. This is an example of 'taking it as it comes', much like my group of teenagers did on our rowboat, rather than approaching the work in the safest, best possible way.

Machinery damages too, are another area of concern for ship owners and hull and machinery insurers. As safety manager, I was investigating a generator breakdown where the cylinder liner had overheated and cracked due to loss of lubrication. The sequence of damage had started when the piston cooling plug loosened and fell out. The cooling oil then drained out, overheating the piston crown, and damaging the engine. The lube oil trip did not stop the unsafe engine operation as the attached pump compensated for the small loss of lube oil.

The engine maker's service letter had advised the piston plug glue be renewed at regular intervals and checked during overhauls. However, if an engineer had never before carried out such a task, how could he know of the potential damage?

The real danger is that unless there is a conscious effort to gain expertise, the human mind tends to cover the skill deficit with misplaced overconfidence!

AN INTENTIONAL APPROACH TO EXPERTISE: A SEA-CHANGE

Experience teaches only the teachable.

– Aldous Huxley, poet

As safety manager, I reviewed numerous industry case studies of groundings and contact damages in ports, which eventually led me to question: What can we do to change the 'take it as it comes' approach? Working with my team, I suggested that our ships' officers approach ship manoeuvres in an *analytical, structured, deliberate,* and *curious* method.

The result? Incidents within the fleet dropped by 90 per cent!

Change is indeed possible.

Within the new approach, navigators *analysed* details and incorporated data such as the ship's characteristics, speed limits, wind and current direction into a *structured* manoeuvring plan template. They *deliberately* practised the manoeuvres in a ship simulator. Adopting a *curious learning* approach, the captain shared notes with pilots and other captains to understand the complexities of the manoeuvre. The navigators were then much more confident when manoeuvring the ship to port. They were taking huge steps towards developing their expertise.

> SKILL IS THE COMBINED FORCE OF EXPERIENCE, INTELLECT, AND PASSION.

When our engineering officers adopted a similar approach towards engine operation and maintenance, they too were rewarded with tangible improvements such as reduced breakdowns and increased efficiency of machinery.

Things to remember:

- Aim to be the best of what you can be. This is the invisible force that will make you an expert. If you can withstand the physical and mental discomforts of sea life to work hard and continue to think deeply about your work, you will gain mastery over the skills you need.

- Practise. Researchers who work with the highly talented musicians and athletes have concluded that practice, rather than just inborn talent, is linked to expert performance. That said, practice needs to be of the right kind and of the right variety, and should be carried out in a deliberate and systematic manner.

- Seek. Experts need to constantly expand their professional knowledge to make them more aware of their area of work. Leaders are learners; they inspire their teams to higher standards of engineering, navigation, and seamanship.

After several years at sea, an experienced officer could end up a non-expert or an expert. We cannot control what kind of experience we will have, but we can definitely maximise how much we learn from our experience. And given that there is no room for error at sea, the seafarer cannot rely on experience alone to guarantee safety at work. It is not just experience, but expertise is the sum of the following four:

1 Experience
2 Deliberate practice
3 Intentional knowledge
4 Focused feedback.

A NEW MODEL OF EXPERTISE: THE CELESTIAL SPHERE

A student acquires Knowledge in the following manner:
One-fourth from the Teacher, one-fourth using his own
intellect, one-fourth through interaction with peers, and
the remaining one-fourth in the course of time.

– Ancient Sanskrit verse

Scholars in ancient India correctly recognised the accumulation of expertise as a systematic, collaborative effort. Several centuries later, in 1955, two American psychologists Joseph Luft (Jo) and Harrington Ingham (Hari), proposed the Johari Window along similar lines to explain our realm of knowledge. Combining ancient wisdom and modern research, I created a **model of expertise** that mariners will find easy to remember and understand.

The inner circle is your area of competency, which you've gained from your studies and time at sea. The outer circle represents expert level skill and knowledge. The gap between competency and expertise

Parani's Porthole Model of Expertise ©

is not a weakness, but rather, an opportunity. Think of it as your untapped potential. The more you expand your inner circle, the closer you get to becoming an expert.

The upper arc, the area 'known by self', represents what you know and what you don't know. It is also the area that you can develop through 'Deliberate Practice' and 'Intentional Knowledge'. As described in the following chapters, you can increase your skills through systematic and varied practice, while increasing your awareness through self-analysis and a habit of curiosity.

The lower arc, the area 'unknown by self', is what you can only know through experience and feedback. Because a mariner *does not even know that he doesn't know these things*, he either has to experience them, which takes time and isn't always positive, or obtain this knowledge from others through 'Focused Feedback'. He can also gain this knowledge when he is trained, coached, or mentored.

You can't predict the challenges you will face or the experiences you'll have at sea, but you can control the other three elements. The more effort you put into Deliberate Practice, Intentional Knowledge and Focused Feedback, the less you'll have to depend on Experience alone for your expertise.

There may not always be a 'boiler expert' to help you at sea, nor will you always have the time. You have to become the Ace that you would like on your team. Maybe even better!

HOW TO BE AN 'ACE'

- Expertise = Experience + Deliberate Practice + Intentional Knowledge + Focused Feedback

- You can't always control your experience, but you can control the other three.

- Parani's Porthole Model of Expertise.

5

DELIBERATE PRACTICE: THE PROPELLER

I hear and I forget. I see and I remember. I do and I understand.

– Confucius, Chinese philosopher, 479 BC

ELLEN MACARTHUR is recognised as one of the world's best solo sailors. Aged just 18, she sailed the entire coast of England. At 24, she showed greatness well beyond her 5'3" stature when she became the youngest sailor to go solo around the world. Three years later, she survived mountainous waves by not sleeping for more than 20 minutes a time while setting her second record: 71 days to circumnavigate the globe.

During her famous voyages she had to single-handedly perform various tasks. Whether it was to repair a broken rudder, sew up damaged sails, or climb a 90-foot mast while the boat lurched through heavy waves. Ellen's expertise and leadership – leadership of *herself*, that is[4] – are proven beyond doubt. She now extends her leadership ashore with her foundation, promoting the circular economy concept aimed at conserving the earth's natural resources.

Just like Ellen, a mariner needs to have super skills, be it navigation, engineering, or cargo work. Ellen worked harder than any of the sailors in her nautical school, and sailed on various kinds of boats to build her expertise. Her long days of deliberate practice helped her instinctively make intelligent decisions in all crucial moments. These decisions led to her resounding success – success that could be measured even at a very young age.

The truth is that practice is *doing*. It's not merely observing. It is not learning about something in theory; it is about rolling up your sleeves and getting your hands dirty. This is what makes you proficient at a task.

---

4 For a full analysis of self-leadership, see Section 2.

But you also need to practise smart. You can't just slip into mindless routine; you need to engage in thoughtful work. And you also need to embrace variety in your tasks to stay engaged and prepared for the unexpected.

When you practise deliberately, you maximise the value you get from your time at sea, and that in turn builds up your expertise. I recommend these two simple strategies for deliberate practice:

1   Maximum practice through maximum performance

2   Widen your practice outside your comfort zone.

MAXIMUM PRACTICE THROUGH MAXIMUM PERFORMANCE: GO FULL REVS!

I'm a greater believer in luck, and I find the harder I work the more I have of it.

– Thomas Jefferson,
3rd American president

Everyone knows a marine engine works best at full revolutions. Go at a slower speed and you gradually decrease its efficiency. Professionals are no different; they work best when delivering maximum performance.

The first element of deliberate practice is hard work. There is simply no substitute for it. You can either put 70 per cent of effort in the job or 100 per cent; you'll eventually notice the difference in the final results. And hard work doesn't mean just working hours on end every day; it means putting our effort into things most needed, even if they're mentally and physically challenging to complete. Putting in your full effort means you leave nothing in reserve. This is the level of effort that provides the thrust to lead by expertise.

Maximising our output helps us think deeply about the work we are doing. It's easy to get confused between being very busy and doing what's important. As a professional, you have to focus on doing what is most important, and on doing it the right way. This deep thinking and hard work gradually builds up those cognitive abilities that are common among expert level performers.

What usually keeps us from giving our 100 per cent on a ship?

A friend of mine, a captain on super tankers, recently emailed me: 'Usually, we go to Japan to discharge, where the charterer's safety officer visits the ship. Everyone is so motivated to present the ship in top shape. But on this trip, we are at a port in a developing country where the safety officer isn't coming. Since there will be no external eyes on the ship, getting my officers and crew motivated to the same level that they would have had in Japan has been a challenge. Now, a slight leak is considered acceptable, or if something is broken and we can manage without it, it is dealt with later. Why do we still need the old carrot and stick approach to keep the ship in good shape? Why don't we set the same standards for every day at work, for every port we visit, through self-motivation? Aren't we supposed to give our best every day?'

MAXIMUM EFFORT MULTIPLIES THE VALUE OF THE EXPERIENCE.

Disruptions in work timings, hectic schedules, overload, multiple demands, complex tasks, unfamiliarity, stress, and poor health are some of the other reasons why we may be underperforming. While it is natural to feel low sometimes, you have a professional responsibility to overcome your feelings and perform at work. If you want to be an expert tomorrow, you have to be a professional today, and a professional is one who will give his very best *even when* he doesn't feel like it!

MAX IT DAILY. CRANK IT UP!

Purpose is what gives life a meaning.

– C H Parkhurst, social reformer

In monotonous jobs such as watch keeping, how do you apply deliberate practice to build expertise? Yes, it's challenging, but it is possible.

Set small, achievable goals. Commend yourself on every ship you pass clear, on every non-GPS[5] position fix plot, on every parameter you see operating correctly in the engine room, on every manual you read, and every maintenance task you complete. This allows you to reflect on your actions, and this process is the key to maximising your experience.

The concern about tiring ourselves is another limiting belief that keeps us from maximum performance. I felt discouraged when I noticed, after having worked hard ship after ship, that the officer I was there to relieve appeared to have gotten by with doing much less work.

---

5 Global Positioning System, using satellites and now the easiest methods of position fixing at sea. Non-GPS position-fixing is more traditional and requires more effort to accomplish.

When my captain heard me grumble about this on a few occasions, he told me not to. When asked why, he said that firstly I didn't know of the issues that officer might have had to deal with on board, and therefore, I couldn't know exactly what he might have achieved; and secondly, it really didn't matter. Working hard at the things that matter always pays.

IT IS BETTER TO WEAR DOWN THAN TO RUST UP!

This is how a true leader increases his physical and mental stamina, thus stretching himself to do more, no matter what the circumstances.

I would later realise that I wasn't going to get a pat on the back immediately, but word about my efforts would eventually get around. I would soon be seen by my peers as a high performer rather than just an average sailor. My hard work not only got me an early promotion, but it also boosted my self-confidence – self-confidence that is key to maximum performance.

Apart from hard work, the manner in which you approach tasks that you dislike can also impact maximum performance. It is perfectly natural, for example, for some to prefer physically demanding tasks over those that require mental focus and an analytical mind. Conversely, there are those who dislike hydraulics maintenance, as it is a messy job that requires long periods of attention. However, in order to gather a wide range of expertise, a professional has to learn to work on all required tasks with equal effectiveness, regardless of personal likes and dislikes.

So how do you get through a task that drains your energy? Firstly, recognise and acknowledge what you dislike, and complete those jobs first. Most people dislike a certain job because they are not knowledgeable enough to do it properly, or they depend on others to do it for them. If you are concerned about whether or not you can complete a task, seek the guidance and support of those around you.

One way to incentivise yourself to do a task you dislike is to treat yourself to a small reward once it is complete. Then, once the energy-draining tasks are done, you begin the tasks you enjoy doing. Over time, when you begin to associate a positive feeling with the tasks you dislike, you will find yourself enjoying both types of tasks. Eventually, as your team sees you strongly committed to all kinds of tasks, you will inspire them by example.

WIDEN YOUR PRACTICE OUTSIDE YOUR COMFORT ZONE

Disturb us, Lord, when we are too well pleased with ourselves, when our dreams have come true because we have dreamed too little, when we arrive safely because we sailed too close to the shore.

– Sir Francis Drake,
second captain to circumnavigate the globe

The pass mark for most competency exams in shipping is usually at least 70 per cent. Not surprising, as the margin of error when these officers go on the ships is low. The final interviews are particularly tough. Stephanos, an engineer and a friend of mine, cleared his exams with amazing ease, while his fellow students had to reappear several times.

I asked Stephanos about the secret of his success, and this is what he had to say: 'We worked on old ships where we had hands-on experience with overhauls, and we handled quite a few tough situations. On the other hand, some of my peers had worked only on newer ships and had read about major maintenance only in theory. We got paid more or less the same, but I worked harder, at the same time learning more.'

Who do you think had more confidence, whether stepping into an interview or an engine room?

Experts hone their skills and expand their knowledge on the whetstone of challenges. It could be an old ship, a new trading area, or working with a difficult colleague. These situations test the limits of our stamina and brainpower, and gradually expand it. Embrace challenges with a positive mind-set, because right outside your comfort zone is a whole new world waiting to be discovered; a sphere of greater expertise.

It has been said time and time again, smooth seas never made a good sailor. Deliberate practice does not just mean doing more of what comes your way but also involves actively seeking out many more things to do. Expand the horizon of your abilities, just as you would see more of the sea when you climb up onto the mast of a ship. Our view of our capabilities, too, is limited by where we stand and what we are currently doing. So push yourself further up, and you will reap the rewards later. Why settle for good when you can be great?

150 PER CENT: THE SAUERKRAUT

Ambition leads me not only farther than any other man has been before me, but as far as I think it possible for man to go.

– Captain James Cook

In the ancient days of exploration, seafarers suffered from scurvy and malnutrition. Captain James Cook, exhibiting another trait of leadership, discovered that sauerkraut (pickled cabbage) prevents both. He made sure his men consumed sauerkraut to stay healthy, which meant his voyages could accomplish more.

Sauerkraut is sour in taste, and seamen found it difficult to eat. But once they discovered its benefits, it became a staple on these ships, helping explorers discover new lands. Extra work, too, is difficult at the beginning, but it carries our expertise beyond our current immediate horizon.

Aiming for 150 per cent means learning and doing beyond our job description. If we don't challenge ourselves, we restrict our expertise and limit our leadership. In fact, doing just enough to keep a job gradually shrinks our capabilities. Unlike non-experts who are satisfied with routines – that is, until a crisis hits – experts constantly tackle problems that challenge their expertise. Organisational psychologists associate this quality with expert-level performers.

Knowing and doing more than the minimum enables leaders to process more data. They develop capabilities to detect, adapt, and respond to situations quicker and better than a non-expert. This is the hallmark of intelligence and expertise.

> EXPERT MINDSET: ASK YOURSELF 'WHAT IS THE ONE NEW THING I LEARNT TODAY?'

Professionals who keep pushing the limits of their skills tend to become experts at what they do. Their initial 150 per cent now becomes the expert's 100 per cent. An engineer who works with the electrical officer can expand his knowledge on control systems, and will be better prepared for the engines of tomorrow.

Even at the top, a captain or chief engineer can find ways in which he can aim for 150 per cent and increase his value. What better way for a leader to inspire their team than to show that they are also willing to do more than their call of duty?

During my command, I regularly asked my navigators to take turns in advanced manoeuvres, such as man-overboard recovery, under my supervision. The result was astounding; the officers became better even at their daily jobs once their intellect had been stimulated and their mental horizons had been expanded.

If you are unfamiliar or uncertain about a new task, just ask! Carry out a risk assessment with more experienced people. If you are shy about asking, ask yourself: 'What's the worst that could happen?' Remember, it is better to be a fool for a minute than ignorant for the rest of your life.

Expanding the horizon does not mean only increasing your view forward, but also means you broaden your perspective all around you. Why? Well, lateral skills also play a large role in shaping your expertise.

LATERAL SKILLS: WIDEN YOUR HORIZON

A man who limits his interests limits his life.

– Vincent Price, actor

Do you know anyone who owns an iPhone? Did you know that its inventor, Steve Jobs, once took a calligraphy course just out of interest? Why would a student of electronics take an arts class which was not part of his graduate programme? At that time, perhaps, no one knew. But the world would later see unique fonts appear on popular Apple products; the typefaces inspired by his calligraphy lessons.

I once took a short typewriting course on one of my vacations; it helped me complete my reports on the ship faster, leaving me with more time for my other duties. It's a very simple example of ways to develop non-core skills to help widen your range of skills and improve your efficiency at work.

> INCREASE THE RANGE OF JOBS YOU CAN DO, WIDEN YOUR HORIZON.

Other examples include speed reading and mathematics, which help high performers process more information quickly and effectively. Enrolling in public speaking classes or improving your presentation skills can make you a better communicator, while photography skills can help you prepare work reports in better light, literally!

Learning hard skills like welding, lathe work or using advanced software applications can make you the 'go-to' person on a ship. A person with a well-rounded personality and skillset makes a valuable leader. Seamanship, after all, has always been about learning skills required at sea.

Ellen MacArthur says, 'The only thing you cannot control is the sea; how you handle the ship and yourself are in your hands.' She showed us all how deliberate practice can enable a person to become a smarter professional in much less time.

DELIBERATE PRACTICE

- Deliberate practice is the propeller that pushes your skills to the maximum.

- Deliberate practice requires 150 per cent at work, even on the most challenging days.

- Go beyond your comfort zone to improve on your skills. If today you are only doing what you were doing yesterday, you are not moving ahead.

- Develop lateral skills.

6

INTENTIONAL KNOWLEDGE: THE RUDDER

He who loves practice without theory is like the sailor who boards ship without a rudder and compass and never knows where he may cast.

– Leonardo da Vinci

ONCE, AS SAFETY MANAGER for the fleet, I investigated an air compressor explosion. Its casing had violently disintegrated like a grenade, and the fragments had flown everywhere like missiles. One of these flying metal pieces had struck a crew member, causing a serious injury. Fortunately, owing to prompt medical attention, he survived the blast.

The tubes in the pressurised air cooler chamber had fractured, and the pressure had been transmitted to the water chamber. The air cooler and the water chambers are designed to work at pressures of 30 and 4 bars respectively. The water chamber has a safety feature to protect it against over-pressurisation. A special bursting disk sacrifices itself at 6 bar, whenever the two chambers are interconnected by accident.

During a previous overhaul, someone had replaced the bursting disk with an unspecified metal sheet, compromising the purpose of this safety mechanism. When the pressure in the water chamber rose to more than it was designed for, the disk did not activate, and the walls of the compressor simply burst.

Replacing the safety disk with an ineffective metal sheet was an act of ignorance. Ignorance on a ship is *not* bliss. No matter how much you practise, you cannot become an expert without the right kind of knowledge. We do not always instinctively know what we need to know, and knowledge doesn't always just come our way. You have to go out there and obtain the right knowledge; this is called Intentional Knowledge.

Intentional knowledge helps you know what you need to know to get the job done properly, to be aware of all the risks that you may face, to consider all possible outcomes, and to take the right actions, every single time. With deep Intentional Knowledge, you are able to pick up every minute detail and accordingly prepare for any job thoroughly. Had the seafarer who replaced the bursting disk possessed this understanding, the accident would not have occurred.

> DON'T WAIT FOR YOUR SHIP OF KNOWLEDGE TO COME TO YOU; SWIM OUT AND BRING IT IN.

DO WE REALLY KNOW ALL THAT WE NEED TO KNOW? THE ALMANAC

To know, is to know that you know nothing. That is the meaning of true knowledge .

– Socrates, Greek philosopher, 400 BC

Sometimes, when I look back at my career, I wonder: 'How did I survive all those years at sea without knowing the things I should have known?'

Research indicates that when people begin working in new positions, they do not know almost 50 per cent of what they really need to know in order to excel at their jobs.[6] Their level of knowledge, acquired in school and from their daily routines at sea, is not enough. Experts are lifelong students who actively seek to learn more. This is why most high performers are self-aware and naturally curious. This is the first step to gaining Intentional Knowledge; realising that no matter which stage of life we are in, there is a lot we do not know.

Intelligence by itself serves no purpose unless it has focus and application. Only when we apply our knowledge do we make best use of our intelligence. It is not just our Intelligence Quotient (IQ) that matters, but also our Intentional Knowledge (IK) that makes us experts.

FIVE POWERFUL SOURCES OF INTENTIONAL KNOWLEDGE THAT CAN HELP BUILD EXPERTISE:

1 Self-analysis
2 Log in your journal

6 Refer to Parani's Porthole Model of Expertise based on the Johari Window, created by American psychologists Joseph Luft and Harrington Ingham.

3   Learn from errors

4   Observe and listen

5   Train to the top.

1 SELF-ANALYSIS: FIND OUT, AND LET YOURSELF KNOW

Millions saw the apple fall, but Newton was the one who asked why.

– Bernard Baruch,
American businessman

As a young seafarer, I remember feeling disoriented at every new workplace. One such place was the mooring stations from where we would send out ten-inch-thick ropes to make the ship fast to a quay. The ropes are strong enough to withstand loads over 150 tonnes, which means when they catch a seafarer's leg, or when they snap, injuries are serious enough to end careers, if not lives.

The first few times that I was at the mooring stations, I felt stupid. I didn't even know where to stand. The supervising senior officer would end up shouting at me, 'Don't stand there, go there. No, not there, not there either. You [insult], do you want to kill yourself?'

This routine repeated itself several times until one day I asked him how I was expected to know what to do. My supervisor wasn't known to give thorough explanations, and he simply handed me a copy of the *Code of Safe Working Practices for Merchant Seamen*. Then he said, 'Find out and let me know.'

The book wonderfully described things like snap back, hawser bights, and reeling methods, with pictures. Suddenly, it all made sense. Mooring accidents are one of the most frequent causes of crew injury, and I am grateful that I learnt the right things the right way, at an early stage.

I would hear the phrase, 'find out and let me know' many times over during my cadet training, and it instilled in me the ability to seek answers for myself. Rather than jumping into unplanned action, I built understanding through gradual self-analysis and by asking the right questions.

WHY, WHAT, AND HOW ARE YOUR BEST SHIPMATES

I keep six honest serving men (they taught me all I knew); their names are What and Why and When and How and Where and Who.

– Rudyard Kipling, author of *The Jungle Book* and *Captains Courageous*

Once, following an alarm, the engine of a ship was opened for investigation. Damage to the crankshaft was revealed. It was serious enough to put the ship out of action for more than a month.

During the investigation, they found rubber particles blocking the lubricating oil system. This meant that the engine was not receiving any lubrication, and that the resulting friction had damaged the moving parts. It became evident that the rubber expansion joints of the lubricating oil piping system had disintegrated, flowed downstream, and blocked the oil nozzles.

On further investigation, it was found that on a previous overhaul, parts meant for the cooling water lines had been wrongly fitted into the lube oil system, leading to its premature collapse. In spite of the fact that the rubber joints were colour-coded to indicate which system they were to be used on, they had been fitted onto the wrong pipes. The crew who had fitted these joints had seen the different coloured spare parts, but had not bothered to ask why. Had they done so, they could have avoided the damage to the main engine.

The first step towards productive self-analysis is to be curious.

'Why are the rubber joints coloured differently?'

'What does the manual say about it?'

'Is there a better way to do it?'

'Am I missing something?'

Analysis deepens understanding and sharpens our skills, and our questions will draw out the purpose of our next actions. Deep knowledge helps us base your professional judgment on solid facts rather than those based just on 'feel', 'intuition,' and 'experience'.

Details matter. One of the first things I would do on joining a ship was to familiarise myself with the details of my ship by reading relevant plans, drawings, and manuals. I would also ask my team to do the same. After all, this ship was going to be our home away from home, and we ought to know it well. Whether it was about setting up equipment for operation, overhauling

A - ALWAYS

S - SEEK

K - KNOWLEDGE

machinery, or reviewing safety precautions, we would read about it and prepare ourselves. We would aim to do it right the first time, and every time.

Never stop questioning. Even in everyday tasks such as engine room rounds, ask yourself:

'Am I checking everything?'

'Am I comparing my notes with those from previous days?'

Your questions keep you alert. Remember: Doing a thing right is simply not enough; understanding why this is the best way to do it helps you identify and resolve issues faster.

Read and analyse. Experts in any field generally read more than non-experts. A good place to start is technical bulletins published by classification societies. Accident investigation reports make us aware of how things can go wrong, and reading these reports helps us learn from other people's mistakes before we make them ourselves. Golden Stripes mariners are well read, which means that they are able to provide useful inputs to their team. Also, isn't sharing knowledge one of the best ways to positively influence and impress your colleagues?

2 LOG IN YOUR JOURNAL

Writing in a journal reminds you of your goals and of your learning in life. It offers a place where you can hold a deliberate, thoughtful conversation with yourself.

– Robin S Sharma, author,
The Monk who Sold his Ferrari

During my first few years at sea as a cadet, I was required to maintain a journal of my observations on the ship. I would record key learning achievements such as celestial observations, sketches of port panoramas, traces of ballast pipelines, and weather conditions. I was encouraged by the captains who monitored my progress, and it eventually became a lifelong habit.

As a second officer, I recorded voyage planning comments such as routes around the Cape of Good Hope to avoid freak waves. As a chief officer, my journal contained information such as characteristics of cargoes, pump performance, and the durability of paints. As a captain, I would log my observations on the ship's manoeuvring characteristics and the peculiarities of harbours.

I still keep a journal. When I look back and review the challenges I have survived, I feel a sense of pride. These journals contain valuable nuggets of information that help me even today. Some of the case studies discussed in this book are from my journals.

Journaling helps you record experiences that you can reflect upon once the day is over. As you write, and later read, your ideas become clearer. You spot trends and patterns. Thus, keeping a journal facilitates clarity of thought and embeds deep knowledge in your long-term memory, all of which is paramount in decision making.

Keeping track of your successes and how you went about achieving them is a great source of inspiration (and ideas) when you need them. If you did it then, you can do it now, and you can do it even better in the future.

It's just as important to track the mistakes you make, because once you've put them down in writing, you'll learn from them and are much less likely ever to make the same mistake again.

3 TO ERR IS HUMAN; TO LEARN FROM IT IS BEING SEA-WISE

Successful engineering is all about understanding how things break or fail.

– Henry Petroski, *To Engineer Is Human*

A long time ago, our captain moved me up from third to second officer. I was understandably elated. Our bulk carrier was anchored off Ko Sichang Island, which is a few miles south-east of Bangkok. There were barges alongside our ship, from which we were loading rice for Brazil. Typically, the second officer is responsible for drawing up voyage plans, and so now I had to make sure we would be on the safest and quickest possible route to South America.

The previous second officer had drawn the route into our current anchorage. I started by simply reversing the track. Subsequently, I asked the captain to cross-check my plan. He had barely started when he stopped, and looked at me with a hard gaze.

'Do you realise that after loading our cargo, the ship will float deeper in the water?' I focused to where he was pointing on the chart. My course would take us over an area shallower than the ship's draught after loading. That track was safe when the ship came in empty and light, but it was unsafe after we were loaded and heavy. Had the captain not spotted my mistake, the ship would have run aground, making us all look very silly.

I felt like banging my head on the ship's gong. I was crushed, and my self-confidence plummeted. I had disappointed myself, and more so my captain who had just promoted me. Struggling to find my voice, I apologised and hoped my previous efforts would overshadow my current mistake. I was relieved when he let me off with a warning. I was even more grateful for his next piece of advice: 'Do not copy blindly; make your own true effort.'

I didn't blame the previous second officer, for the current voyage plan was my responsibility. Nor did I try to ignore or find an excuse for my mistake. The captain, like most people, was smart enough, and he would have known if I had tried to cover my back. Good thing I didn't, because it would only have eroded my credibility as an officer. Instead, I chose to learn from my failure and move on, never to repeat it. Today, I look at all my tasks, even routine ones, with careful eyes. This experience not only helped me improve the quality of my own work but also to verify the work of my team.

Don't get me wrong; you don't have to be making all these mistakes yourself. As a sea-wise mariner, you will learn more from the mistakes of others. Keep your eyes and ears open. Listen to the experiences of others. Read circulars, safety alerts, and investigation reports.[7] If you have not experienced something bad yet, that doesn't mean it cannot (though I pray it won't) happen to you.

Unfortunately, like history, many accidents repeat themselves. Do you remember the air-compressor explosion I mentioned at the beginning of this chapter? During my research, I discovered that there at least three known cases of similar damage due to incorrect installation of safety discs. I only wish the engineer had read about these accidents before the overhaul.

Another example is the large number of accidents during lifeboat drills which kill seafarers every year. Very often the reason is improper operation of the hook-release gear. So, why wait to learn the hard way? Errors of others should serve as a warning so that we can avoid the same mistakes. Remember: to err is human, to *learn* from it is being sea-wise.

4 OBSERVE AND LISTEN: SEA-SPONGE

Observe, record, tabulate, communicate. Use your five senses.
Learn to see, learn to hear, learn to feel, learn to smell, and
know that by practice alone you can become expert

– Dr William Osler, medical training pioneer

In Chapter 1, I narrated how a pilot saved our ship from grounding after we lost the steering. He reacted to the situation calmly,

---

7 Refer to the useful websites listed at the end of this book.

instinctively made the right decisions, and inspired the rest of us to rally around him. Watching him in action inspired me to be a better mariner. I observed knowledge transform into action that day, and he had showed me how it's done.

Studies have shown that people learn a lot by observing the actions of others, and the consequences of those actions. When you listen to different views and experiences, they become part of your memory. This memory helps you respond to unfamiliar situations that you may face in future. Observe and listen; become a sea sponge. Analyse and absorb the information around you, and incorporate it into your expertise.

> LISTEN TO OTHERS, EACH PERSON HAS A UNIQUE EXPERIENCE TO SHARE.

Experts rarely thrive in isolation, and most professionals help each other raise awareness through a mutual sharing of ideas and experience. On a ship, this can be through casual conversations or organised meetings. Invite each colleague to speak about the technical problems that they encountered at work and how they solved them. Ask others to provide their inputs if they previously experienced something similar and approached it differently. Create the right learning culture on a ship, and you will have a ship full of experts.

You can continue learning ashore too. Mariners can join professional associations such as the Nautical Institute or the Institute of Marine Engineering, Science and Technology. These associations always promote expertise through their publications and seminars. They also form a nurturing community that allows mariners to tap into a wider network of knowledge.

5 TRAINING: THE GRINDSTONE

Training increases the probability of learning, and learning increases the probability of job performance.

– Frank J Landy, organisational psychologist

You know by now that I first grounded my boat at the age of 16.[8] The second time was ten years later, off the Berendrecht Locks at Antwerp. To align the ship to the locks, I had applied helm to counteract the strong currents flowing up the River Schelde. However, as the forward section passed the wall, the currents acted only on the stern, while

8 Chapter 3.

my counter helm was making the bow move rapidly towards the wall adjoining the locks. Before I had time to understand what was happening, the ship hit the wall with considerable impact. I was embarrassed, of course, but I was thankful this grounding was in a ship simulator.

After the instructor explained to me the nuances of ship handling in such situations, I repeated the exercise, this time successfully bringing the ship through the locks and to the berth. I had learnt this manoeuvre earlier in theory, but I only understood it during training. This training ensured that I did not make the same mistake on an actual ship.

Training also helped me narrow my experience gap by focusing on certain skills and providing real-time feedback. It helped me push the boundaries of my own performance. Simulators can train a navigator for ice conditions long before he sees his first ice edge. They can train an engineer on advanced automation, which improves his chances of success when faced with a malfunction at sea. On any given day, a well-trained employee is more valuable to his employer than one who is not. Embrace any training activity as an investment in yourself, and not as a burden.

Research confirms that the desired effectiveness of any training is achieved only after multiple sessions, and seldom after just a day's training. It is, therefore, a continuous process that you should repeat at regular intervals, or else the knowledge and skills will slowly dissipate to their original levels. Training can be in the form of simulators, classroom sessions, computer-based modules, drills, or workshops.

Mariners, like most professionals, are also knowledge workers. Your minds are your tools, and training is the grindstone that keeps it sharp. No matter how good you are today, more training will only make you better.

Another advantage is that during training, we take our minds off our daily work and intentionally focus on the accumulation of knowledge and on doing things the right way.

Being a trainer also helps develop Intentional Knowledge. In fact, being able to teach is a mark of true knowledge. Anyone can become a trainer. I once asked our second officer to conduct a training session on the operation of the ship's radio equipment. After the session, he came up to me and admitted that this opportunity had helped him refresh his memory. To prepare for it, he had to research and be ready for questions. This exercise upgraded his knowledge, and he felt proud demonstrating it. In this context, training can be a win-win situation for all.

Intentional knowledge is knowing the ocean before the voyage. It is knowing more through analysis, reflection, and training. The more you know, the better you can lead.

WHAT'S YOUR IK?

- IK is as important as IQ.
- Intentional Knowledge is gained in five ways;
    1. Self-analysis, by reading and reflecting.
    2. Journaling.
    3. Learning from mistakes.
    4. Observing and listening.
    5. Receiving and providing training.

FOCUSED FEEDBACK: THE SOUNDING LINE

Feedback is the breakfast of champions.

– Ken Blanchard, management expert

ONE OF MY STRENGTHS is my ability to stay calm in any situation. When faced with a challenge, I usually switch to problem-solving mode rather than become frustrated by it. I thought that this was something everyone did, until one of my colleagues complimented me on it. My cool and decisive demeanour was deemed a valuable trait at work. Needless to say, I was super-pleased with myself.

Until he kept talking.

He said dryly that I could be a better listener. It seems I would go into solution mode mid-way through a conversation, which meant I wasn't listening fully, nor was I picking up details. I was already preparing an answer in my head, and that interfered with my listening. This time, though, I listened carefully and reflected on what he had just said. I thanked my colleague for his feedback. I was glad that he had pointed out a flaw which could have become a handicap later on in my career. Gradually and consciously, I worked on enhancing my listening skills, which are a key both to good leadership and to build expertise.

Professional feedback that I have received over the years has helped me develop my skills and calibrate my mindset. Research shows that most of us begin our careers not knowing many of the things we need to know. This 'Unknown by Self' area (refer Porthole Model of Expertise) is filled through experience and focused feedback. And while the experience that we accumulate is not always in our control, we can surely develop the skill and mind-set to receive feedback.

On a ship, we measure the level of fuel in the tanks with a sounding line. Similarly, feedback makes us aware of our expertise, or lack thereof. My ship handling skills for manoeuvring into lock-gates were improved thanks to my trainer in the simulator. When I made a mistake with the voyage plan, my captain's feedback helped me approach any work with fresh eyes.

Over the last decade, I have been leading teams in various departments. My position requires me to provide feedback to my colleagues, both ashore and at sea, on almost a daily basis. Here are my tips on handling feedback:

- No one is perfect.
- Look at feedback as an opportunity to improve. Remember, someone wants you to be a champion!
- Don't always dismiss feedback as criticism, or take it personally.
- Be open to feedback from anyone, even from your subordinates.
- Actively seek feedback to receive more.
- Ask specific questions to get focused feedback.
- Giving and receiving feedback is a skill that can be learnt and improved with practice.

ARE YOU RECEIVING THE FEEDBACK CLEARLY? UNTANGLE THE LINE

If you spend more time asking appropriate questions rather than giving answers or opinions, your listening skills will increase.

– Brian Koslow, businessman and coach

On one of my voyages as captain, the technical superintendent for my ship made a harsh comment about the maintenance of our ship's tanks. He pointed out that the paint had not been prepared and applied properly. I was embarrassed because deep down I knew that he was right.

The chief engineer was also present during this exchange. Having seen my reaction, he later asked me, 'Did you receive the feedback clearly?'

Noticing that I was confused by his question, he continued with a smile, 'I saw you get upset because of the superintendent's abruptness. So I thought your emotions might be stopping you from listening clearly'.

He was on a roll: 'Hear what he has to say, not how he says it. Remember, he is upset about the situation and not necessarily at you.

Don't take it personally'. This single piece of advice has helped me throughout my career, particularly when personality clashes and bruised egos could have gotten in the way of good judgment.

So how do you handle feedback in the best way possible?

The answer is quite simple, really. When the *ultimate objective of all feedback* is to increase or improve your expertise, you stop judging the intention behind the comment. This is the sign of a mature professional.

Take emotion out of the equation, just as you untangle a sounding line before using it. No one is perfect, but if we're willing to try, we can be better tomorrow than we were yesterday, and receiving feedback is one way to achieve it. The problem in most cases is that the very thought of someone pointing out a fault can make us angry, suspicious, and resentful. In order for the feedback to be effective, you must learn to conquer your ego. Because, at the end of the day, your expertise needs to be more comprehensive and powerful than your ego. Resisting, denying, or avoiding feedback is like closing a window and shutting out the light.

The best way to control your emotions during feedback is to actively ask for it. The more you ask, the more you'll become used to it, and the less painful it will become. If you can replace your negative reaction to feedback with a positive one, half your journey is complete.

ACTIVELY ASKING FOR FEEDBACK: ECHO-SOUNDER

Ask for guidance from someone senior enough to provide it. Asking for education is not a sign of weakness. People love to be asked for their opinion; seek them out. Sometimes it is hard to know what is it that you don't know, but you sure won't find out quickly if you don't ask enough questions.

– Rear Admiral Casey Coane,
US Navy, *Saltwater Leadership*

When I asked my captain for his feedback about my passage plan,[9] I was hoping to hear praise but I was also prepared for criticism. I knew the captain would check my work, but my asking for his feedback made him comfortable in doing so. Asking for feedback isn't a sign of weakness; it is a sign of respect, and those who are asked will nearly always appreciate and welcome the opportunity to give it. If I had not asked for feedback, the captain would have most likely rejected

---

9 See story in 'Intentional Knowledge: 3: To err is human'.

my plan without much explanation. Instead, he even handed me a valuable piece of advice for life. My request was specific, and so was his feedback, which helped me improve my passage planning skills. Had I not asked, I would never have known what it was that I needed to know at the time. This is why asking for feedback is such a useful emotional and practical skill.

For an echo sounder to work, it has to first transmit a pulse of sound. The pulse then travels downward through the water, bounces off the seabed, and is received back by the device, thus being able to calculate the depth of water under the ship. Good feedback works just like an echo sounder. When you initiate, or ask, you should get the information you are looking for.

Actively seeking feedback helps you focus on how to do better. When you make the first effort to ask, you have better control over the feedback session. Ask questions that give you specific answers. If the feedback you receive is unclear, ask for a clarification. For example:

'Can you give me an example where I should have …?', or

'What in your opinion should I have…?'

Do not assume that asking questions will expose your lack of knowledge. The real danger is in getting so comfortable with what we do not know that we stop asking questions altogether. On the other hand, someone who is eager to help you will appreciate your humility when you ask for feedback.

TO ASK, OR NOT TO ASK? SOUND PULSE

He who asks is a fool for five minutes, but he who does not ask remains a fool forever.

– Chinese proverb

After a seminar on captain–pilot communication, Captain Ed Heijmans shared an interesting observation with me. He had served at sea for several years, first as a captain and then as a harbour pilot. 'As a captain, I was uncomfortable asking the pilot about manoeuvres because I was afraid he might be offended. Later, as a pilot, I often wondered why captains didn't ask enough questions.'

It is true that some people become impatient, or do not respond well when asked questions, but that is their problem. Your responsibility is to know, and to ask if you don't. A bit of thick skin is useful sometimes, especially in professional interactions. If you find yourself debating whether to ask or not to ask a question, ask!

Do we need to worry that others will laugh at our questions or call us ignorant? Not at all. It doesn't matter. What matters is that we need to grow our expertise. Without questions, we get no answers. Without answers, our minds struggle for clarity. Without clarity, our judgment is affected. Without a good sense of judgment, we may not make the right decision at a critical time.

The seabed does not reveal by itself the depth of water over it. That is determined alone by an echo sounder. Likewise, people are reluctant to offer unsolicited comments until something goes wrong. However, by then it is often too late. So send out that sound pulse and ask. Be active even when seeking feedback during performance appraisals. It takes the stress out of the process. Appraisals are a great way to decrease our 'Unknown by Self' area and build our expertise.

And be open to feedback from anyone: your bosses, peers, and subordinates. Or it could be someone you work with on a project: a pilot, an engine technician, or a surveyor. If you adopt a mind-set that you can learn something from everyone, you will become genuinely interested in seeking expertise-building feedback.
Remember: feedback opens the door to the unknown, but you have to turn the door handle by asking the right questions.

FEEDS ON FEEDBACK

- Feedback is the only active way to learn about things we didn't know we were unaware of.

- Make feedback work for you by actively asking for it.

- Ask specific questions to receive clear feedback.

- If you don't fully understand the feedback, respond with open-ended questions .

- Separate emotions from information when receiving feedback.

- Don't be shy; directness in asking for feedback is the mark of a good leader.

EXPERTISE

- *Self-Analysis*
- *Log in your Journal*
- *Learn from Mistakes*
- *Observe & Listen*
- *Train*

KNOWN BY SELF

- *Max it daily!*
- *Go for 150%*
- *Lateral skills*

Deliberate Practice

Intentional Knowledge

COMPETENCY

- *Time*
- *Maximise experience through Deliberate Practice, Intentional Knowledge and Focused Feedback.*

Experience

Focused Feedback

UNKNOWN BY SELF

- *Actively Ask Feedback*
- *Untangle Emotions*

A MODEL FOR BUILDING EXPERTISE - THE KEEL OF LEADERSHIP!

Experience is a good teacher, but it takes time and you have no control over it. However, you can maximise your experience through deliberate practice, and you can maximise its value through Intentional Knowledge and focused feedback. Record your experience in your journal, analyse it, learn from your mistakes, and be open to feedback. Remember this, to help you become an expert leader.

8

LEAD YOURSELF: THE HULL OF LEADERSHIP

The problem in my life and other people's lives is not the absence of knowing what to do but the absence of doing it.

– Peter F Drucker, management expert

CAPTAIN EDWARD J SMITH was 62 when he took command of the *Titanic* on its maiden voyage. He was considered an expert and was a commodore at the White Star Line. He perished a hero, saving lives until his last breath – but he also failed to bring his ship safely to New York.

Even in the opinion of Sir Ernest Shackleton, the *Titanic* should have slowed down when it received reports of navigational dangers close to its intended track. Radars to detect ice in the dark had not yet been invented, and slowing down would have given the ship ample time to spot and avoid the iceberg.

Irrespective of how much we know, our actions connect our expertise to results. They determine whether the ship reaches port safely or sinks to the bottom of the ocean.

In Chapter 3, I established that expertise is the keel of leadership. But a keel alone does not make a ship. Expertise tells us what to do, how to do it, and why it needs to be done. Motivation is what makes us *want* to do it, and alertness is what makes us *able* to do it, day after day. We need all these elements to lead ourselves. Leading ourselves is as much about knowing our stuff, as making sure that we are *doing* what we need to do.

Lead yourself to be goal-oriented. Our motivation directly influences the effort we put into the safety of our ship, the maintenance of its machinery, and into finding solutions to problems. Our efforts to prioritise effectively, to develop a strong team on the ship, and to sustain a robust safety culture determine whether or not seafarers return home safely.

Lead yourself to be detail-oriented. Our motivation determines how careful we are with every task we perform. A single nut out of place can cause an engine breakdown. An incorrect setting on an electronic chart will fail to alert you to a potential grounding. Such focus and attention comes with the drive to complete the job as perfectly as humanly possible.

LEAD YOURSELF BEFORE YOU CAN LEAD OTHERS.

Lead yourself before you think of leading others. Leaders lead best by example, and by energising others. If you display inappropriate behaviour or show indecision at every turn, how can a team look up to you for direction? If you do not radiate positive energy yourself, how can you charge up your team? If you violate procedures, even occasionally, how can you expect others to follow them? If you lack self-confidence, how can you make others feel comfortable with your leadership?

Leading yourself is all about you. You are the person everyone on the ship and ashore count on to make it happen. It is *you*, and only you, who is responsible for what you are able to accomplish.

Often, we excuse ourselves by thinking that everyone else is the problem. We either label our superiors as 'too demanding', our subordinates as 'lacking commitment', or life in general as 'too stressful'. This approach only puts external elements in control of your life and success. Instead, take charge of your work and life, and control the outcome. You can surely achieve more when you have the required ability, have a positive attitude, remain constantly alert, and demonstrate commitment to your job throughout your career.

LEAD YOURSELF DESPITE CHALLENGES: RIDE THE WAVES

Poor practices resulted in mistakes, mistakes resulted in poor morale, and poor morale resulted in avoiding initiative and going into a survival mode of doing only what was absolutely necessary.

– Captain David Marquet,
Turn the Ship Around!

Bad news, just like good tidings, is part of the ebb and flow of life, usually beyond our control. The second officer on the chemical tanker *Ovit* was visibly upset when he heard that his relief from Hamburg had been cancelled. His family would have to wait a few more days to see him. The captain, sensing his disappointment, felt that he might not be in a good frame of mind. As a caution, he asked the third officer to assist the second officer with the voyage plan.

The third officer completed the plan, but it contained a fatal flaw: it would take the ship over a dangerous reef. The second officer, whose job was to prepare the passage plan, was not feeling motivated enough to verify his subordinate's work.

During the voyage, the chief officer was content to follow the set route and was not even aware of the danger until 19 minutes *after* the ship had run aground on the Varne Bank in the Dover Straits. While the chief officer was physically present on watch, he was most likely elsewhere mentally, content that the ship was on autopilot.

The captain too, for unexplained reasons, appeared to display a low level of motivation at work. He had not reported defects on the electronic chart display to his head office, nor had he attempted to fix them himself. He never checked if the third officer, who was preparing a voyage plan for the first time, had done a proper job. What's even more surprising is that the captain did not come onto the bridge for over a quarter of an hour after the ship had grounded to investigate why the ship had stopped in the middle of the Dover Straits.

The team aboard the *Ovit*, though fully qualified and certified, were neither alert nor motivated enough to ensure that the ship safely completed its voyage from Rotterdam to Brindisi. Fortunately, the consequences of this grounding were limited to loss of the hull paint in the keel area, diversion to Dover for underwater inspection, and a corresponding loss of revenue.

It is difficult to hold off personal issues from affecting our work. But it must be done if we are to succeed as leaders. There may be instances where we may not feel at our best, such as in this case where the officer's relief was delayed. We may feel disturbed when we hear of our loved ones at home being sick. At times, even rough seas can bring on low morale and stress. However, feeling demotivated will not speed up an expected result; instead, it will make work seem miserable. Poor morale causes us to make mistakes, and the sea does not always forgive our faults.

Complacency is a key ingredient in disasters. The *Titanic* was going at full steam across the Atlantic, as was the practice in those days. The belief was that nothing could go wrong, and the ship

POOR
MOTIVATION AND
ALERTNESS CAUSE
COMPLACENCY.

had famously been labelled 'unsinkable'. Complacency comes with lack of motivation and alertness and, as in that case, it may even cost over 1,000 lives.

You are the only one *you* have control over. Your professional conduct, winning habits, and self-confidence are all under your control. By developing the right attitude, discipline and skills, you can positively influence yourself and the people around you to deliver positive outcomes – outcomes that might someday include saved lives.

Therefore, lead yourself to be always alert. Only when you are in top physical and mental shape can you have the stamina to be constantly attentive. At sea, every wave brings with it fresh challenges; stay alert and sail through to success.

Leading yourself also means holding yourself responsible to a high standard of professional behaviour. Disciplining yourself means being in conscious control of your emotions, state of alertness, habits, and stamina at work. Here are my four practical techniques for the Golden Stripes mariner to lead himself:

1 Lead your motivation
2 Lead your attention
3 Lead your habits
4 Lead your mind-body machine.

LEAD YOURSELF TO BECOME A BETTER YOU!

LEAD YOURSELF

- Only when you lead with expertise and lead yourself can you lead others.

- The 3 As of Achievement = Ability + Attitude + Alertness

- Lack of motivation + lack of alertness = complacency

- Leading yourself means being in conscious control of your actions.

9

LEAD YOUR MOTIVATION: THE MOTOR

Why are we Masters of our Fate, the captains of our souls?
Because we have the power to control our thoughts, our attitudes.

– Alfred A Montapert,
The Supreme Philosophy of Life

WHEN ONE OF THE UNITS on a ship's main engine stopped during a manoeuvre, our team was called in to investigate. We opened the engine and found that the exhaust cam shaft had been running without adequate lubrication.

The water content in the lube oil was at least 50 times more than the recommended 0.1 per cent because leaks from the cooling water lines had found their way into the lubricating system. This made the lubricating oil unfit, allowing metal parts to wear down.

There were more issues in the engine room. The water-in-lube oil monitor and the lube oil purifiers had not been operational for almost a month before the incident. The exhaust valve's air spring pressure settings were also incorrect, causing a higher load on the cam. Overall, the engine had suffered from neglect.

We had known the chief engineer for many years. He was known to be a technically-skilled and hard-working man. So it was out of character for him to ignore something like this. Embarrassed and apologetic, he said, 'I don't know what happened to me in this tenure. I have let many things slip. I had some lower back pain, but this was not the main problem. I guess, more than that, I let my previous success make me a bit indifferent to my work.'

At times, even the best of us can lose focus of what is important. Unfortunately, the ship and the sea do not empathise

MOTIVATION IS WHAT MAKES US OVERCOME INERTIA, AND ACT.

with our problems. When we ignore the ship, we suffer and may feel the consequences immediately.

Just like barnacles attach themselves to the side of a ship over time and slow it down, mariners too may suffer from a loss of drive at work. The reason may be poor health, interpersonal conflicts, troubles back home, or just plain indifference. It is during these times that we just go through the motions at work. We become prone to accept unsafe situations. We ignore machinery settings. We lack initiative. Instead of solving problems, we let them persist. But the ship always has a way to let you know.

Motivation is what gives us the energy to tackle everyday problems. It is the motor which drives our leadership. It is easy to keep your motivation up when things are going well, but how can you be at your best, consistently, every floating minute?

HOW DO WE MOTIVATE OURSELVES DAILY? MOTOR POWER

People often say that motivation doesn't last. Well, neither does bathing – that's why we recommend it daily.

– Zig Ziglar, US Navy, WW II veteran

A leader does not wait to be motivated by others. He generates his own source of motivation. No one else has the power or responsibility to motivate you; you are the best person to motivate yourself.

For those who believe in a higher power, prayer is one sure way to stay strong at sea. The Almighty, of course, helps those who help themselves. External incentives such as promotions or clearing a vetting inspection can get the adrenaline flowing, but these do not last long. The best motivation comes from within.

In high-risk industries such as aviation, marine, medicine, and mining, the standards of safety are high. Everyone expects the ship's crew to behave professionally, day after day. Our behaviour, however, is influenced by our emotions.

Our feelings are what drive us to perform, but they can also cloud our thoughts and distract us from our focus. Leading ourselves means staying positive and learning to manage negative emotions.

THE BEST MOTIVATION COMES FROM WITHIN.

YOU CAN MASTER SELF-MOTIVATION WITH THESE FIVE POWERFUL TECHNIQUES:

1. Build strong self-confidence
2. Draw inspiration
3. Let your body motivate your mind
4. Set your own goals
5. Conquer demotivation.

1 BUILD STRONG SELF-CONFIDENCE: THE BOW

A strong, positive self-image is the best possible preparation
for success.

– Joyce Brothers, psychologist

The Ambrose Light beacon marked the entrance of New York Harbour for 41 years, shining a guiding light to ships bound for the Big Apple; that is, until 2007, when the oil tanker *Axel Spirit* crashed into it, damaging it beyond repair. The captain had misjudged the ship's approach, assuming that the beacon was farther than it actually was. The second officer, who was also on the wheelhouse, knew that a collision was imminent, but he did not alert the captain in time. If he had clearly voiced his concern, the Ambrose Light would still be standing.

In most such cases, lack of self-confidence makes us reluctant to speak up, particularly to our superiors. Taking initiative, displaying assertiveness, and making decisions require faith in our own abilities. This belief is vital to build self-confidence.

Self-confidence is to a mariner what a bow is to the ship. The bow pierces through rough seas and ice, making way for the rest of the ship. Self-confidence leads our abilities, making headway through challenges and ambiguities. It is critical in our journey to success.

YOU WILL BECOME WHAT YOU WANT TO BE.

How can you build your confidence?

Visualise. Ask yourself, 'How do I want to see myself now and in the future?' You could visualise yourself as 'an expert, as a trusted colleague, and a mentor'. Or simply, 'The best there is!', or 'A Golden Stripes mariner'.

The more you see yourself as a success in the future, the greater are the chances that you will take the steps necessary to make that vision a reality. You will develop the drive to work hard and push yourself. You will meet people who you think can help your career goals with their inputs.

Instead of just ending up where life takes you, take control. Your image is in your hands. Shape your vision as you progress through your career. But always have a vision for yourself. You alone can paint your world in hues of success.

Assess your personality type. There are several books and free online self-assessment tests that can help you analyse your strengths and areas for improvement. Some even assess what motivates you, while others, if you dig deep enough, can assess traits such as decisiveness, adaptability, directness, rule acceptance, and the ability to be part of a team. It is true that your personality is influenced by factors such as your upbringing, education, family, and the nature of your job. However, you can make a conscious effort to subdue your weaknesses and build on your strengths, eventually becoming the person you want to be.

Keep a list of your strengths, even small ones like punctuality or neatness. Every small positive attribute adds to your personality. List your personal and professional achievements in life, including even your high school science quiz trophy. I keep my achievements in a journal and refer to it periodically. It never fails to boost my spirits when I'm having a bad day. Focusing on our strengths motivates us to achieve more.

2 FIND YOUR INSPIRATION - IT'S EVERYWHERE: STAR SIGHT

People never improve unless they look to some standard or example higher and better than themselves.

– Tyron Edwards, theologian

Find some role models. Chief Engineer Petar Becić was twice my age when I sailed with him, but he also had double my energy. When I felt lethargic on some days, I only had to think of him to motivate myself. When faced with a challenge, I often think of my role models and ask myself, 'What would he/she have done in this situation?'

Role models help us to learn more, and inspire us to do better. They may possess one or more leadership qualities we want to be able to display. If someone else can do it, so can you. When we were younger, we all had role models: parents, teachers, athletes, explorers, or astronauts, to name a few. These people inspire us to dream big, work hard, and display positive virtues.

Read positive material every day. There are many inspirational books, such as *South* by Sir Ernest Shackleton and *It's Your Ship* by Captain Michael D Abrashoff.

Movies too have inspiring stories to tell, whether it is the quick thinking of the crew of the *Maersk Alabama* in the movie *Captain Phillips*, the determination of a survivor at sea in *Unbroken*, or the skill of the captains in *Master and Commander: The Far Side of the World*. The quality of your life will be influenced by the books you read, and the positive stories you come across.

3 LET YOUR BODY MOTIVATE YOUR MIND: THE GOVERNOR

A good stance and posture reflect a proper state of mind.

– Morihei Ueshiba, Founder of Aikido
(a modern Japanese martial art)

Have you been reading this book in a crowded and uncomfortable space? Or are you leaning back in your private space, perhaps a favourite chair, and feeling relaxed?

Research reveals that good posture not only affects how others perceive you but also impacts your internal body chemistry. A good posture is beneficial to your spine and your core, and it stimulates the brain to generate feelings of positivity. On the other hand, slouching and hunched shoulders lower feelings of self-confidence.

Smiling eases stress. Frowning only elevates feelings of anger and anxiety. A purposeful and unhurried stride keeps you alert. Strong postures increase the levels of testosterone and lower the levels of the stress-producing hormone, cortisol. When you're less stressed, you feel more in control and make better decisions.

If the officers on the bridge of the *Axel Spirit* had felt confident enough, they would have alerted the captain before he made a major error, and the Ambrose Light would still be guiding ships into New York!

What about what we wear? Don't we all feel good when we wear a crisp shirt? It is a wonder how simple things like neat clothes can help boost motivation. Research shows that people listen more carefully when receiving advice or instructions from a person wearing a uniform or a well-pressed suit, and that makes you more effective at your workplace. Yes, your overalls are going to get dirty but you can always start your day with clean ones.

Looking good and feeling good go hand-in-hand. When you feel good, you do good. Looking good is not only limited to our posture and our clothes; regular exercise, while helping you to stay in shape, also releases 'feel good' hormones called endorphins. These hormones boost feelings of motivation, which later show in your confident body language. When your colleagues see the confidence in your eyes, your stride, and the way you dress and carry yourself, they feel confident that they can trust in your leadership.

4 SET YOUR OWN GOALS: VOYAGE PLAN

Continuous effort – not strength or intelligence – is the key to unlocking our potential.

– Winston Churchill, twice prime minister of the United Kingdom, and first lord of the Admiralty 1939–1940

A friend of mine had this to say about one of the officers on his ship: 'As the entire ship was preparing for the inspection, he took it too easy and resisted any efforts to help him improve his focus. After the inspection, he had a long list of defects to fix within a day, but he couldn't do it alone. The company reprimanded the officer for his lack of professionalism'.

When we don't have our own goals, we allow others to set them for us.

Leading ourselves also means that we have to set our own goals. When you set your goals, you own the motivation to reach them, and you increase the chances of achieving them. If you have successfully overhauled a pump, or completed a project in record time, congratulate yourself for a job well done. You are a good judge of your work; don't wait for someone to notice it, at least not always. If you take it further and stretch yourself every day, the process of setting and achieving your goals becomes even more meaningful. How about completing that overhaul an hour earlier than the last time? That extra bit, no matter how small, will help keep you motivated and energised.

When you are setting your goals, remember that you are striving to be better than you were yesterday. Hold yourself responsible for an

WHEN YOU OWN YOUR GOALS, YOU OWN YOUR MOTIVATION.

excellent standard. When you believe that you consistently excel in your goals, it becomes a self-fulfilling prophecy.

5 CONQUER DEMOTIVATION: RIDE OUT THE STORM

Pray, and let God worry.

– Martin Luther, German theologian

The chief officer's heart sank when he received a disturbing email from his partner back home. His mind went blank and he stopped paying attention to navigation. He forgot to change the course at two critical points, and now the container ship was heading towards the Egyptian coast at a speed of 21 knots. The chief officer was alone in the wheelhouse

For almost half an hour, the Vessel Traffic frantically called the *Norfolk Express* on the radio to warn them of the danger, but the chief officer was simply too demotivated to notice. Only when the ship hit the shallows did he realise that they were aground.

The chief officer's demotivated behaviour did not solve his personal problem; it only made things worse. Now not only did he have a personal problem, he would also have to answer for his professional negligence. Unfortunately for him, he was compelled to quit his career at sea after this incident. Keeping away from demotivation is as important as staying motivated.

Demotivators at work are a fact of life. Sleep deprivation, sickness, conflict with a colleague, or criticism can all drain your energy and enthusiasm. While we may not be able to control disheartening news from home, we can definitely control our reaction to it. When at sea, beating demotivation is key to survival.

The first step in conquering demotivation is recognising that you are not in a good state of mind. Let your colleagues take over or support you in your duties until you have found time to process the bad news and strengthen your mind. Better to ask for help now than later, when it might be too late!

Next, realise that no amount of worry, anger or complaining is going to solve the problem; it will only make it worse. Worry is like the ship's heave and sway; it may be movement, but it does not take the ship forward. If a loved one is sick, the best you can do while you are away at sea is to offer

CONQUER DEMOTIVATION BEFORE IT DEFEATS YOU.

words of comfort. If it is a conflict, don't take it personally; resolve it through dialogue. Resentment harms you and makes you lose interest in your work. You can indeed pray for things to get better, but stop worrying. Don't ask why, but ask yourself how you can solve it.

Admiral Horatio Nelson of the British Royal Navy is remembered for the heroic battles he fought, despite losing the use of his right eye and right hand. As a modern professional, you are very unlikely indeed to have to suffer to this extent, but you can still give your best even when you do not feel like it.

You have the privilege of working on a multi-million dollar ship with dozens of shipmates depending on you for their safety. Instead of saying 'you have to work', tell yourself that you '*get* to work' in such a position of responsibility. A simple change in the way you think can put you in a more positive frame of mind.

A Golden Stripes mariner needs to have the mental stamina to put his feelings aside and focus on the safety of his team. Use your will power to act strong irrespective of how you feel. Stay busy; let your discipline and habits conquer any demotivation.

You cannot navigate a ship when towed, or when pushed from behind. External motivation does not always help. Internal motivation is like *having your own* motor power. Harness yours and you can choose where you want to go.

STAY MOTIVATED

- Motivation is what makes us work effectively.

- Leaders are responsible for their own motivation.

- Practical techniques for healthy motivation include:

  1   building strong self-confidence

  2   drawing inspiration

  3   letting your body motivate your mind

  4   setting your own goals

  5   conquering demotivation.

- Conquer demotivation by (a) realising you are not feeling good, (b) informing others if you need help, (c) understanding that worry will not help, and (d) putting your immediate responsibility first.

- You can control how you feel, and you can definitely control how you act.

10

LEAD YOUR ATTENTION: THE RADAR

The error of one moment becomes the sorrow of a whole life.

– Chinese proverb

FOR THE *MAERSK KENDAL*, it was supposed to be another routine approach to Singapore. Both the captain and the chief officer on the bridge had worked on similar container ships in the past. They had manoeuvred into Singapore several times. Both were highly qualified and motivated individuals. Yet, the ship ran aground on the Monggok Sebarok reef just off the harbour, ripping its forward keel plate.

The captain was engrossed in keeping up with the schedule, picking up the inbound pilot, and avoiding collision with the outbound ships. The chief officer was busy answering the radio and monitoring the ship's position. Neither of them realised that the ship was moving faster than it should have been. The high speed meant that each navigator was forced to process more information in less time. The overload of information meant that they lost focus of a critical detail: they were going to run out of water soon!

If they had simply reduced the speed earlier, both navigators would have had time to fully grasp what was going on and avoid the grounding.

In open waters, ten minutes of inattention can create dangerous situations. During manoeuvring in closed waters, ten seconds of distraction is enough to cause an accident. The speed of your response to an oil-mist detector alarm or a high temperature alarm decides how long, if at all, your ship will be disabled at sea. Your attention needs to be where it needs to be, all the time.

WHEN DISTRACTIONS COMPETE FOR YOUR ATTENTION: CLUTTER

Law: Any occurrence requiring undivided attention will be accompanied by a compelling distraction.

– Robert Bloch, author

Arnel is quite the capable third engineer, and a great shipmate to work with. I sailed with him a few years ago. He shared a very interesting story at the dinner table.

'I was fitting a new flexible fuel line in the generator. Once both ends were connected, I took a step back and had a look. Something was not right. Was it the angle of the pipes? I wanted to refer to the maintenance manual. As I reached for it, the phone rang. The chief engineer wanted the main engines to be prepared for departure. I made a mental note to check the pipe drawings later. In the end, I got so busy with other work that I forgot to look it up.'

Arnel paused a bit and shook his head, apparently with a tinge of regret: 'While we were at sea, we needed to put the generator in use. There seemed to be no problem so I assumed everything was all right. But it wasn't. Weeks later, one of the fuel pipe connections failed due to a pressure surge. Oil from the pipe sprayed on to a hot manifold, causing a fire.

'It was then that I remembered that I had forgotten to check the manual. When I finally read it, I realised that the fuel pipes had been fitted at the wrong angle. This had made them susceptible to a pressure surge. The error was not intentional but I was distracted by other demands.'

> WE WILL ALWAYS HAVE 100 THINGS TO DO, YET TIME FOR ONLY 10; THIS IS A FACT OF LIFE. KNOW THIS AND MANAGE YOUR PRIORITIES.

Fifty-six per cent of all engine room fires result from a fuel line leaking onto a hot surface. In this case, when Arnel had to complete the maintenance under time-pressure, the circumstances forced an error. We will always have multiple demands on our time and energy. Our mind is being overfed with information all the time, just as the radar screen gets cluttered with echoes of waves and rain. In such situations, it is usually a challenge to return our focus back to work after losing it even for a few seconds.

But again, just as you would tune a radar to shut out the clutter echoes, you can tune your mind to minimise the effect of distractions.

HOW ATTENTION FADES AWAY DURING ROUTINES: HAZE

This thing we call luck is merely professionalism and attention to detail, it's your awareness of everything that is going on around you.

– Stephen Coonts, *The Intruders*

People wonder how ships collide with each other when there are thousands of miles of water around them. We can find some answers from the collision of the refrigerated cargo ship *Timor Stream* and the bulk carrier *Seagate* in open seas under perfect visibility.

The captain of the *Timor Stream* was alone on his ship's bridge. He had a quick look at the horizon; it was clear. So he thought it was a good time to finish some paperwork. He got engrossed in preparing his reports and did not look outside for the next 40 minutes.

On the *Seagate*, the chief officer was relaxed. It was a long passage from Beaumont, US, to Lagos, Nigeria. Everything looked fine. His thoughts were disturbed by the lookout, who showed him the silhouette of the *Timor Stream* on the starboard side. He had a cursory look at the ship, and decided it was overtaking.

If he had bothered to calculate the angle of approach of the *Timor Stream*, he would have realised the ship was crossing and on a collision course. Instead, he went back to his reverie. The other ship was seen as a nuisance rather than a sign for action.

Both the navigators ignored the other's ship. They realised the true danger only seconds before impact. The force of the collision flooded the *Seagate*'s engine room and smashed part of the accommodation. Luckily, no one was injured.

KEEP YOUR RADAR OF ALERTNESS ALWAYS ON.

Research points out that after periods of inactivity, the mind becomes less sensitive to signals. A short inactive period lulled the navigators' minds on both ships into a false sense of security. The captain on the *Timor Stream* thought it acceptable to work on his reports rather than look out of the bridge windows.

On the *Seagate*, nothing remarkable had happened over the last hour of the chief officer's watch, so he stopped paying attention. It is not uncommon for people to subconsciously lower their alertness when they believe nothing much will happen. So when a crisis hits, their response becomes inadequate. Just like haze can dull the appearance of the horizon, routine can dull the mind. On a ship, a dull mind which is slow to respond can have damaging and possibly fatal, million-dollar consequences.

Take intentional control of your attention so you mind stays clear of the haze. Be alert and stay focused, so you can detect and react in time.

HERE ARE FIVE PRACTICAL TECHNIQUES TO LEAD YOUR ATTENTION:

1 Give yourself time
2 Prepare to be distracted, so you are not
3 Stay mindfully manual
4 Engage your senses
5 Focus your vision.

1 GIVE YOURSELF TIME: LEEWAY

Take time for all things: great haste makes great waste.

– Benjamin Franklin. Among many accomplishments,
he discovered the Gulf Stream and the sea-anchor

If the *Maersk Kendal* had been slower, the senior officers would have had more time to appreciate and react to the developing danger. If my friend Arnel had given himself more time to prepare and carry out maintenance, he would have fitted the fuel pipe the right way. Whenever possible, give yourself sufficient time.

Planning realistically helps. When calculating your ETA (estimated time of arrival), take into account conditions such as rough weather, traffic, and fog that you may encounter. When preparing for maintenance, allow sufficient time for the work, breaks, and surprises. When you work without being rushed, your mind focuses on doing the job properly even if you have to spend some time on distractions that could not have been foreseen.

2 PREPARE TO BE DISTRACTED, SO YOU ARE NOT: RED BRIDGE

By prevailing over all obstacles and distractions, one may unfailingly arrive at his chosen goal or destination.

– Christopher Columbus, explorer, navigator

The ferry *Pride of Canterbury* was waiting outside the port of Dover for the weather to subside so they could enter. On the bridge, the navigators received a call from a truck driver on board. He wanted to know if he could start his engine to maintain the temperature of his cooled cargo. The officers consulted among themselves and allowed him to do so.

Minutes later, the truck's exhaust fumes set off the smoke detectors.

Curious passengers and crew started calling the bridge to find out if there was a fire on board. The navigators felt they had to respond to the alarms and calls and so they left their conning positions. In doing so, they forgot about the nearby wreck they had earlier seen marked on the chart and the ship sailed over the old wreckage, damaging the propellers and the rudder. Eventually, the ship was out of action for several weeks, and losses would total over one million US dollars.

The *Pride of Canterbury's* officers were not prepared for distractions. They did not use the ship's 'Red Bridge' system to discourage non-essential communication while manoeuvring. If the navigators had intentionally chosen their focus, they would not have been distracted from their main task.

What do you do when you have to bunker fuel, complete a survey, pick up stores, repair a pump, and complete cargo operations, all within a port stay of 30 hours?

Distractions, multiple demands, and conflicting priorities are all part of life. In trying to attend to *all* of them, we may lose track of one. And we lose situational awareness. Most ship crews prepare for an emergency, but how many prepare for stressful situations? Most of us respond to such situations by experience or by intuition, but seldom by design. Being mentally prepared for the unexpected allows us to be in a state of alertness.

Preparation eases pressure. When you are prepared, you assess potential issues, prioritise, and focus on the primary task past all distractions. When you prepare, you can call on more resources to help manage the multiple demands, or delay decision making on secondary issues. Choose which issues to pay attention to, and which tasks to delegate. These are not easy decisions to make; nevertheless, we must make them.

Know what to do when your attention is distracted. Sometimes we start thinking of the next task and we lose focus on the one at hand. While we cannot always stop our thoughts from wandering, we can always make a conscious effort to bring them back to our work.

3 STAY MINDFULLY MANUAL: HAND STEERING

A hundred years ago, a ship's survival depended almost solely on the competence of her master and on his constant alertness to every hint of change in the weather. Ceaseless vigilance in watching and interpreting signs, plus a philosophy of taking no risk in which there was little to gain and much to be lost, was what enabled him to survive. Both seniors and juniors alike must realize that in bad weather, as in most other situations, safety and fatal hazard are not separated by any sharp boundary line, but shade gradually from one into the other.

– Admiral Chester A. Nimitz, US Navy

Trouble often comes without prior notice. I know this from experience, particularly this time when we narrowly avoided certain disaster.

We were entering a port through a narrow but deep natural channel. A pilot with good local knowledge was helping us manoeuvre into the harbour. He had been on our ship on previous occasions and we knew he was extremely capable. The ship had to maintain a robust speed to counteract the treacherous currents that crisscrossed the channel. Everything was going as planned. We were now approaching a turn at the end of the buoyed channel.

Unexpectedly, the pilot ordered the rudder to the left to turn; he was turning one buoy too soon! He was apparently unaware of his error, even as the ship started turning towards a knife-edged reef. At 13 knots, the ship's bottom would be slit open like an orange peel.

Within a fraction of a second, both the chief officer and I noticed the fatal error. We sprang into action, ordering the ship back onto its track within the channel. The ship stopped swinging towards the reef and came back, heading into safety. The pilot was startled; he realised his mistake. Once he recovered, he was thankful that we had been alert. Though we knew we had had a near miss, we were pleased that we had been mindfully attentive when it was most required.

Most situations at work *do not* announce themselves with an alarm or a warning sign. The transition from normal to dangerous can occur within seconds. On that day we had no warning, nor could we have guessed that the pilot would lose focus; it was only our alertness that led us back to safety. Had our minds phased into autopilot, had we eased into thinking that the pilot had everything under control, we would have realised too late that the ship was in danger.

Routine work can also make us go into 'auto' mode. A UK marine accident investigation report described how a chief officer who was climbing up a platform to operate a hatch-cover lost his footing, fell overboard, and died. Human tendency sometimes takes us into 'auto' mode as we're performing routine tasks such as watch-keeping or climbing ladders. It is no wonder that slips, trips, and falls cause the greatest number of crew injuries on ships.

This 'auto' mode lets us speak on phones while driving a car, or lets our thoughts wander while we're keeping a navigational lookout. We go through the motions without focusing, preoccupied with other thoughts. But the simplest of jobs can end abruptly with the severest of consequences. So mind your mind; keep it on manual.

Staying 'mindfully manual' means being consciously aware of what is going on, and this takes effort. When the pilot had asked for the ship to turn to the left, I knew it was a wrong order as I was the one counting down the buoys before which we could swing the ship. The chief officer also knew, as he had been watching the electronic track line on the radar.

MIND YOUR MIND; STAY ON MANUAL RATHER THAN ON AUTO.

Research finds that 'pattern-interrupts' help break the 'auto' state of the mind. If you stimulate your attention and question what you are observing, you can avoid slipping into auto mode. Questions such as 'What next?', 'What if …?', or 'Am I sure?' help keep the mind in manual mode. Ticking off a checklist as you complete tasks, or marking positions on the chart as you progress through a manoeuvre, are also effective ways to mitigate 'mind wandering'. When looking at parameters of machinery and displayed information in the engine room, compare with past records of the same variables. Talking to your team also helps; depending on your position in the team, confirm or ask about the progress of the task. It helps you and your team to stay on 'manual'. On that day, I was counting down the channel buoys in my mind, at times even saying it out aloud. I had also calculated the time at which we would be making the turn, which was another way to stay mindfully manual.

During rounds or on watch, simple things like varying your walking speed or taking a different route helps you keep your attention on 'manual'. Walking instead of only sitting during watches helps with blood circulation and keeps the brain alert.

Stay attentive, mindfully, intentionally.

4 ENGAGE YOUR SENSES: BAROMETER

All credibility, all good conscience, all evidence of truth come only from the senses.

– Friedrich Nietzsche,
philosopher

On that day, my senses also played a role in preventing the grounding in the channel. The channel was so narrow that we could not have depended on the GPS alone to sound the warning. It would have been too late. A part of my brain was also aware of the subtle change in the colour of the sea over the reef, and the orientation of the landmarks. These sensory references supported my split-second conclusion that the ship was in immediate danger.

ENGAGE YOUR ATTENTION WITH YOUR SENSES.

Making full use of our senses sharpens our instincts. A red sky in the morning can confirm the barometer's reading that bad weather is on the way. But you don't need to be over-dependent on instruments. A pump running dry can be identified by its sound and vibration; the smell of fire indicates trouble even before the alarm goes off. Simply observing the colour of the smoke from the funnel can indicate trouble with engines and boilers. An electric motor with hot bearings can indicate anything from shaft misalignment or overtight belts to damaged bearings. Tune into your senses at all times, and you will be rewarded with a sixth sense that can forewarn you when things may be going wrong.

Sensory scanning also breaks the dullness of routine. Scanning helps you observe and not just see; listen and not just hear; feel and not just be present. During a navigation watch, focus on each section of the horizon and tell yourself whether or not it is clear.

Our second engineer once narrowly prevented a starting air explosion. He did so simply by responding to the hot surface of a supply pipe from the air rail. When taking engine room rounds, focus on each gauge to evaluate that the reading is what it should be. Check if multiple sensors agree. Make a conscious attempt to feel the temperature and the vibration. Feel your ship so it starts talking to you.

5 FOCUS YOUR VISION: BINOCULARS

If a man does not know to what port he is steering, no wind is favourable to him.

– Seneca, Roman philosopher, 4 BC

A friend of mine, a chief engineer, shared with me a story about how he learned about the miracle of focused work.

A superintendent was visiting his ship for a routine inspection. After exchanging greetings, he went down to the engine room and took a walk on top of the main engine cylinder heads. When he got down, he said, 'You have cooling water leaks from seven out of ten units!' After seeing that it was indeed true, my friend wondered why he had not observed this earlier. In spite of taking rounds of the engine room every day for the past three months, he had simply not seen the leaks. If he had focused effectively, he could have spotted and rectified the problem much earlier.

Leading your attention also means focusing your vision. How many times have we wondered why some inspectors find more deficiencies within an hour than we can find over few months on the ship? Why does the pilot notice the ship's drift before we do? It's not just because of their expertise; it's also because of their *intense focus*.

We see finer details when we focus the binoculars. Similarly, we can detect work issues more effectively when we focus our attention. Focus makes a good professional even more successful at what they do.

Why are our minds not naturally focused? Our surroundings, modern media, and people around us all feed us an endless stream of information. The mind struggles to sort out the useful information from the clutter. Our brain power is stretched thin trying to multitask rather than to focus.

FOCUS TUNES OUR SENSES AND OUR SUBCONSCIOUS, WHILE MAGNIFYING THE EFFORTS OF THE CONSCIOUS.

It takes not more than five minutes each time to condition our minds to focus clearly on the task ahead of us. Here are some pointers to get you started.

Visualise. Before approaching a port, spend five minutes visualising the features of the harbour and the steps of your manoeuvre. Before an overhaul, visualise the various steps of the procedure. Visualise the result of a successful outcome. Research has proven that spending time visualising a task increases our focus, sharpens our concentration, eliminates distractions, and fine tunes our reaction time.

Get 'in the zone'. Five minutes of visualisation puts you 'in the zone'. The 'zone' is where every sense of your body tunes into your work. Visualisation harnesses the power of your subconscious mind to work for you while performing the task. While your conscious brain receives information from the senses, the subconscious works simultaneously to process all this information and reduces reaction time. Preparing to focus by getting 'in the zone' charges you up emotionally, mentally, and physically for what you are about to do.

Prepare. Five minutes of preparation before an inspection makes better use of the time. My chief engineer friend realised that he had been going on daily general rounds, yet he had failed to notice problems that were in plain sight. On the other hand, the superintendent knew where the weak spots would usually be and this is why he planned to start his inspection with the cylinder heads, thus finding the leaks.

On advice from the superintendent, my friend started devoting at least five minutes to preparation, wherein he studied manuals and referred to previous reports. He then gave himself at least half an hour from his daily routine for at least one focused inspection. During these 30 minutes, his mind would change from the 'open focus' of daily life to a 'narrow, selective focus' for this planned task. When he arrived at a site, his inspection was now like a surgical procedure – precise, efficient, and effective.

> FIVE MINUTES OF FOCUS BEFORE A TASK IS LIKE TAKING AIM BEFORE YOU SHOOT.

Give special focus to unfamiliar tasks. Several mistakes occur when engineers independently carry out a maintenance routine for the first time, or when a captain is manoeuvring into an unfamiliar port. Without focus and preparation, we tend to compensate our knowledge gaps with assumptions. Assumption is the reef unseen to the eye but ever ready to puncture the hull of leadership. Be attentive, and you can avoid disaster.

One last thought. Your physical and mental health determine how attentive you are. Sufficient rest aids concentration. A concept in yoga says that a straight spine keeps the brain alert. On long watches or extended periods of work, regular water intake or hot beverages help keep lethargy at bay. If you're taking medication that induces drowsiness, inform your colleagues of your condition. When your body feels good, your mind is attentive.

Your ability to lead your attention enhances your success at work. Strive to get an A for attention.

HAVE YOU PAID ATTENTION?

- Our attention is intentional. Lead it to where it needs to be.

- Distraction happens without us realising it. Manage it before it manages you.

- Both dynamic situations and routine tasks challenge our alertness.

- How to get an A for Attention:

    1   give yourself time to be attentive

    2   prepare to be distracted, so you are not

    3   stay 'mindfully manual'

    4   engage your senses

    5   focus your vision.

- Stay 'mindfully manual' by (a) being aware of the dynamic environment around you; (b) not going into 'auto' mode; and (c) using 'pattern interrupts'.

- Spend 5 minutes to focus your attention by (a) visualising; (b) getting in the zone; and (c) preparing to focus. Don't forget to give special focus to unfamiliar tasks.

- 30 minutes a day for at least one focused task helps you make better use of your time.

11

YOUR HABITS - YOUR MASTS

Watch your thoughts, for they become words.

Watch your words, for they become actions.

Watch your actions, for they become habits.

Watch your habits, for they become character.

Watch your character, for it becomes your destiny.

– Lao Tzu, Chinese philosopher, 6 BC

ROALD AMUNDSEN OF NORWAY is often referred to as 'the last of the Vikings'. He took human civilisation a giant step forward when he became the first man to reach the South Pole.

Captain Amundsen was a strong, tall man. Born in 1872, into a family of Norwegian merchant sea captains and prosperous ship-owners, he cultivated his habits early in life. As a youth he insisted on sleeping with the windows open even during the icy winters to help condition himself for a life of polar exploration.

He believed in preparation. He selected the ship for his expedition carefully. The *Fram* was a round-bottomed ship and would rise and sit on the ice instead of being crushed by it. He also picked Greenland huskies for their proven ability to pull sleds on ice.

Captain Roald Amundsen also believed in time management. He knew that keeping a consistent routine and being disciplined were key to keeping his voyages on track and making them a success. He and his men followed his strict timings for work, meals, and even social interaction.

Captain Amundsen was an organised man. From assigning his crew duties for cleaning their living quarters, to making one man responsible for constantly reorganising and reducing the weights on the sleighs, he made sure that every task was carried out in a systematic manner. He had organised supplies beforehand, which would help them make the final push to the South Pole. Perhaps the most amazing example of his organisation and leadership skills is that he ensured a sauna was available outside their hut in Antarctica. He knew his team need to keep a high morale, and for that they needed to stay warm!

Each of Captain Amundsen's habits played an instrumental role in shaping his glorious destiny. We may not all face the extreme dangers that Amundsen and his men did, but even on a modern ship there's no shortage of challenges. We may have the knowledge, but it is our habits that help us turn our knowledge, one small step at a time, into our everyday actions.

One of the most recognisable features on a ship is its mast; it indicates the size of the ship and the direction in which it is headed. Habits are like a person's mast; they are the most visible indication of a mariner's professionalism and leadership. Good habits are instantly recognisable. A leader who wants to influence himself and his team must first build a strong mast of habits.

If you want to achieve excellence in big things, develop good habits, even in small things. Sustained habits form self-discipline. Discipline does not limit you, but in fact allows you to be your best, even in the most difficult circumstances.

THREE TOP HABITS THAT SEASONED MARINERS SUCH AS CAPTAIN ROALD AMUNDSEN ARE KNOWN TO DISPLAY:

1   Planning
2   Time management
3   Being organised.

1 PLANNING: CHART YOUR COURSE

When you fail to plan, you plan to fail.

– Benjamin Franklin

Tristan da Cunha is perhaps the world's remotest inhabited group of islands. It lies almost in the middle of the South Atlantic Ocean, with an overall area of 80 square miles. In the islands are only 80 families, whose members carry one of the seven surnames: Glass, Green, Hagan, Lavarello, Repetto, Rogers, and Swain. The island is like a needle in the huge haystack of the world's second largest ocean. Yet, one fine day in March 2011, just before the break of dawn, a large bulk carrier crashed onto its rocky shores. Why?

Poor planning.

The *Olivia* was sailing from Brazil to China with a cargo of bulk soybeans. While this is a typical bulk carrier route, no large-scale charts were made available for this leg of the voyage. Instead, blank plotting charts were used until the grounding.

There was no plan for cross-verification, so the second officer's error in plotting the waypoints went unnoticed. Neither did the navigators have a mental picture of their current navigation area, so when the island actually showed up on the radar, they assumed it to be a rain cloud. The captain did not plan to be on the bridge when the ship would be passing through this group of islands. The navigator on the bridge realised that the ship was in danger only when he heard the shrieking of steel on the rocks.

There were no plans for critical activities on this ship; they were created as a formality to reconcile the paperwork, and not as habit. This made the difference between reaching China and losing the ship in the middle of the Atlantic.

Foresight is an essence of leadership. Foresight is anticipating a future situation, a future problem, or a future requirement. A Golden Stripes mariner cannot afford to be surprised or be caught unawares. You gain foresight through the process of planning, and not necessarily from the plan itself.

When you plan, you evaluate, prioritise, communicate, and have greater control of the situation. In fact, I would say that on a ship, good planning is 90 per cent of a job well done.

Unfortunately, as several accidents like the *Olivia* reveal, a good number of mariners consider planning a waste of time. It's considered impractical because it's often difficult to finish every planned task. But the fact is, more tasks are completed successfully with planning than without.

As crewing and training manager for about 8,000 seafarers, I am tasked with reviewing performance-appraisal reports. A weakness that I see most frequently reported is an officer's inability to effectively prioritise and plan tasks. Master the art of planning, and you will see an amazing increase in your own and your team's output.

FORESIGHT IS GAINED THROUGH THE PROCESS OF PLANNING, AND NOT NECESSARILY IN THE PLAN ITSELF.

Lack of planning leads to waste of time and energy, and increases stress later. Our movements begin to resemble the roll and pitch of the ship – lateral movement but no headway. Each one of us can identify people suffering from this 'roll and pitch' syndrome; they appear to be busy all the time but are seldom effective. They could have rolled up sleeves, dirty overalls, and cluttered tables, and are too busy to do anything more, but they still struggle to get things done. It is easy to spend too much time on routine matters such as (and especially) emails at the expense of high-priority tasks such as taking effective engine room rounds.

Most people plan their education, career, and family. Governments plan economic policies, military strategy, and infrastructure. Planning should be an inescapable part of our lives which, when done as a matter of habit, only improves how we do what we do.

WHEN TO PLAN

Before anything else, preparation is the key to success.

– Alexander Graham Bell,
inventor of the telephone and hydrofoils

Different tasks require different timelines for planning, for example:

- Four to six months, for major overhauls, docking, ports for loading spares, or preparing for winter navigation;
- Monthly, for maintenance routines and emergency equipment trials;
- Weekly, to consolidate the monthly plan and break it down into daily chunks of work. Weekly planning also provides for a Plan-B, in case rain or heavy weather disturbs our original plan.
- Daily, mostly consisting of risk assessment and the coordination of activities with other departments or shore offices. It is not necessary to plan for every minute of the day; a plan for about two-thirds of your working hours is practical and allows for disruptions or delays.

In addition:

- Project plans may be required when we prepare for ship modifications, installation of new systems, and gearing up the ship for new trading areas.

- Voyage plans and cargo plans should be made not just because regulations require it, but mainly because they help us complete it safely and in time.

In short, every job needs a plan, else we risk crashing into our own needle in the haystack.

HOW TO PLAN

The best way to keep something bad from happening is to see it ahead of time, and you can't see it if you refuse to face the possibility.

– William S Burroughs

Create a 'mental motion picture'. The idea of planning is to visualise the flow of future events, account for possible challenges, and prepare an action plan to succeed. Anticipation helps us make the right choices, especially in unfamiliar situations, and prepare for the unexpected.

Planning is a proven success strategy for top performers, whether an athlete, a surgeon, or a mariner. Simply projecting in your mind how you will remove the turbocharger or pick up the pilot will increase your chances of doing it right.

When planning, remember that you are doing it for your own sake. Don't prepare plans just to satisfy regulations or 'fill in' the paperwork; do it to prepare yourself and your team for the task. Look before you leap. An ideal plan always asks questions such as:

'What is the best way to do it?'

'What are the risks?'

'What are the alternatives?'

'Why do we need to do this?'

'When and where do we do it?'

'Who does what?'

'How and when to communicate?'

And finally, 'What do we do if things go wrong?'

Keep the plan dynamic! Plan, but be ready to adapt. You must be flexible enough to take into account the changing needs and priorities on a ship. Is the wave

PLANNING
VISUALISE
ASK QUESTIONS
COMMUNICATE
EXECUTE
REVIEW THE PLAN
KEEP IT DYNAMIC

height more than you expected? Or is there more traffic than you expected? In either case, reduce your speed, even if you didn't plan for it. Reality can be unpredictable, so be ready for surprises.

Next, discuss the plan with your team who will do what, how, and by when, and issue guidelines on when reporting or further communication is required.

Finally, execute the plan unless there is a compelling reason not to. It can be tempting to put off a meeting or a drill, but true discipline is in sticking to your intentions. After all, plans are only intentions until they are transformed into good work!

2 TIME MANAGEMENT: TIME AND TIDE WAIT FOR NO SEAMAN

A well-organized life finds time for everything.

– Anonymous

Captain Robert Falcon Scott reached the South Pole just about a month after Captain Roald Amundsen. Scott narrowly lost the race to be the first man to reach the South Pole. To make matters worse, the delay caused his team to run into inclement weather and soon out of provisions. They lost their way back and perished before they could return to base.

If not for the wrong timing, history would have been written differently. Time and tide indeed, wait for no seaman, even one as great as Captain Scott.

Time is a resource. Leaders are resourceful. Managing oneself is about the effective use of our time, and putting the priorities in the right order. On the other hand, when we find ourselves short of time we feel stressed and make more mistakes.

Since we always have tasks and people awaiting our attention, managing time is also about managing our priorities. There are only 24 hours in a day, and successful time management is getting the priorities right. Consider the following when managing your time:

- Watch keepers on duty should spend no less than 90 per cent of their time on lookout and primary duties of the watch. The 90/10 time-organisation rule helps us avoid distractions such as paperwork and phone calls.

- Set aside time so that you are available for critical tasks such as approaching port and engine maintenance. Plan your rest before the scheduled procedure so that you are fresh and alert to carry out the critical tasks.

- Assign time-slots for routine activities such as checking emails, daily rounds, meetings and personal care. Reach an agreement with your colleagues ashore if checking emails at a predetermined three times a day is sufficient. Set aside time for exercise, recreation, and rest so that you can recharge for the next day.

- Plan the remainder of your day in the order of priority. I find using A and B lists in my diary very useful in this regard. List A tasks are those that must be completed the same day. List B tasks are usually minor, such as reviewing files or working on parts of a long-term task. List B also helps to fill in unexpected time that becomes available, such as a delayed departure that opens up a few hours. While I try as hard as I can to complete list B, I don't lose sleep over it. When in doubt, I consult with my superiors on which items to prioritise.

- Allot time for each item on the A list using the two-thirds principle. Based on one hour, allow 40 minutes for the task and 20 minutes to transition to the next task. This allows for unexpected interruptions and personal breaks.

- Delegate whenever possible. If you try juggling all the tasks yourself, there is a real chance of erring in one.

Show your commitment by being on time whether for work or for meals. Coming on watch five minutes early is a sign of professionalism on ships. Having a schedule shows that you respect your own time, and that of others. Managing your time is managing your resources. Planning your time helps you achieve more.

3 BEING ORGANISED: STAY SHIPSHAPE

For every minute spent organizing, an hour is gained.

– Benjamin Franklin

Some of life's valuable lessons are learnt not in classrooms but in unlikely, faraway places. We were loading copper ingots at a small port in Peru. Most locals there either worked at the nearby mine or fished. The harbour was originally designed for trawlers, which meant our ship's cranes were the only means available to load cargo. I recall that we bought fresh octopus and mangoes for our crew, but that's not the only reason I remember this port.

It was late Friday evening and one of the crane pulleys broke down, bringing cargo operations to a standstill. After opening up the pulley block, we saw that we needed to replace its roller bearings. We were confident that we could get the crane back to work within the hour as our records showed that we had two spares. Imagine our surprise when we opened the spare parts store to find that the box was empty! These were special bearings from Sweden that you wouldn't find in a small town in Peru; considering that the warehouses in Europe were shut for the weekend, it could take at least a week to fly the spares in.

While the rest of us searched frantically for the missing parts, the captain called the previous chief officer who was home on vacation. He appeared relieved as he said 'look in the fitter's workshop'. Easier said than done. After about another hour of turning the place upside down, we found the bearing tucked away inside a drawer, wrapped in an unmarked cloth.

EVERYTHING MUST HAVE AND MUST BE IN ITS PLACE.

We had lost a few hours, but we managed to change the broken part before midnight. The delay cost us a few thousand dollars. But it could have been worse and cost us much more, had the bearing not been found on board. We considered ourselves lucky to escape with a small price for not being organised.

The spares had apparently been stored in the wrong place when they arrived on board. Later, we found out the second bearing had already been used, but the inventory hadn't been updated accordingly. So, instead of focusing on the task at hand, we had been distracted by piece after piece of information, until we had everything we needed to move on.

Whether it's a spare, a tool, a document, a spreadsheet, or a manual, being organised demonstrates professionalism and helps your day move smoothly.

- Organise your workspace to keep your mind clear. Use boxes, trays, and folders (both paper and electronic). Dedicate some time every week to streamline and declutter.

- Clean up after your work. Clear your table or workbench at the end of the day. Spend the last ten minutes of today organising for tomorrow.

- Label and identify. Oil spills due to the operation of wrong (unmarked) valves are quite common. Ships have lost power after the wrong circuit breakers were operated. Fatal explosions have occurred when crew welded above a fuel tank, thinking it was a ballast water tank. On ships where crews change every few weeks, maintaining these labels is vital. Label your files clearly. Don't forget your tools; racks with shadow markings help us easily figure out what goes where.

- Keep tools and spares ready for use. I've seen main engine repairs delayed just because the hydraulic jacks for opening the cylinder head nuts were found defective. Or because fuel injectors were not tested and ready to be used as spares. Generator connecting rods have been damaged because the torsion wrenches used during maintenance were uncalibrated. As a result, the bolts had been incorrectly fastened, and they came undone during operation.

- Put things back in their place immediately. Don't leave them out to sort through later because a pileup will soon become unmanageable. Or worse, a safety hazard.

- Record promptly. Update the spares list as soon as you use that roller bearing. Make an entry in the oil record book after a sludge transfer. Do it when the event is still fresh in your mind.

- Reply to emails immediately as soon as you read them. If you wait longer, you will waste time in reading it a second time before replying. If you need more information, let the sender know by when you intend to respond. Back up your computer hard drives regularly.

- Keep a pocket notebook. It helps to jot things down when you observe a defect during your rounds, or when you get an idea that needs following up. Take notes during meetings and discussions. Don't rely on your mind alone by committing everything to memory, because that is more stressful than taking notes.

Staying organised is being in control. It is staying shipshape.

HABITS FOR SUCCESSFUL LEADERS

- Three top habits for professionals: (i) planning, (ii) time-management,and (iii) being organised.

- The process of planning is more important than having a plan. The six steps are: (i) visualisation, (ii) asking questions, (iii) communicating the plan, (iv) execution, (v) reviewing, and (vi) keeping it dynamic.

- Time management is about managing priorities.

- Allot times for tasks using the two-thirds principle, which gives you sufficient time to cope with the unexpected delays and distractions.

- A and B work list help reduce stress while managing priorities.

- Being organised keeps the mind clear. A leader needs clarity of mind to focus on problems and make decisions.

12

YOUR MIND-BODY MACHINE

Physical fitness is not only one of the most important keys to a healthy body; it is the basis of dynamic and creative intellectual activity.

– John F Kennedy, US president.

As the commanding officer of a wrecked torpedo boat, he rescued a burnt crewmember by swimming for hours with the lifejacket strap clenched between his teeth.

CAPTAIN JOSEPH J HAZELWOOD was considered to be a talented master by his company when he was given command of the *Exxon Valdez*. His technical skills and shipboard coordination skills were appraised to be of excellent standard. However, on 23rd March 1989, his mind-body machine failed him when the ship was departing from a port in Alaska.

He had consumed a few drinks earlier in the day while on shore leave, and was not in the best condition during the ship's departure. He was also going through a divorce at that time, and four years earlier had undergone treatment for alcoholism and mental depression. All these factors compounded and influenced his judgment that fateful day. Captain Hazelwood put the ship on autopilot and on full speed. He then chose to delegate a tricky manoeuvre in the congested Valdez Narrows to the third officer, who was relatively inexperienced.

Third Officer Gregory Cousins had never before executed such a challenging manoeuvre. The heavy tanker overshot a turn in the narrow channel and ran aground on a reef. Several of its cargo tanks were punctured, spilling over 11 million barrels of crude oil. The environmental damage caused by this

WE NEED OUR MIND-BODY MACHINE TO PROPEL OUR LEADERSHIP.

incident has been documented in numerous books, articles, and films. Exxon spent over 2 billion US dollars, including about 90 million US dollars in criminal fines, because of the damage. All this due to the ship captain's poor execution of duties.

In spite of his expertise, Captain Hazelwood failed to command his mind-body machine on that day. Even a professional at his level cannot perform his best unless his mind and body are in perfect harmony.

MOST HEALTH PROBLEMS CAN BE AVOIDED THROUGH OUR OWN CARE.

It is your responsibility, and yours alone, to take care of your mind-body machine. Your mental and physical abilities are the best resources under your control that enable you to meet the daily demands of ship life. How else can you stand navigation watches for hours, inspect cargo holds, withstand extreme temperatures in the engine room, or work on an icy or hot deck?

To lead yourself, you need to put an effort into keeping your mind and body in top form. Otherwise, you can't tap into either resource when you need it the most. It's like a ship's engine, where you have to be careful what fuel you burn and what routine maintenance you carry out, and ensure you operate it under the correct parameters. It's also a matter of self-discipline and investing in yourself. After all, if you don't invest in yourself, who else will?

WHEN THE ENGINE FAILS: BODY TROUBLES

And your body is the harp of your soul,

And it is yours to bring forth sweet music from it or confused sounds.

– Khalil Gibran, poet, 1883–1931

The 61-year-old chief engineer of the bulk carrier *Apollo* had a history of diabetes, hypertension, and kidney problems. His medications had helped him pass the medical examination ashore. But he still had to climb the ladder to board his ship that was at anchor off Hong Kong. After climbing just six steps, he was unable to go any further. He had a heart attack and fell into the water. Although immediate assistance was provided, unfortunately he passed away.

This story isn't unique; heart attacks are the major cause of deaths among seafarers. Other common serious medical troubles include hypertension, back pain, diabetes and kidney stones. Alcoholism and smoking, and their side effects have also prematurely ended many bright careers.

But with the right care, most lifestyle diseases are preventable. Don't wait until you're in mid-career or for a mid-life 'muffin top' to appear. Start early and stay disciplined. Our body has an easier time staying in shape when we start caring for it in our younger years, and not just when we find ourselves facing health troubles. Just like a ship's engine, planned routine maintenance is better than breakdown maintenance.

After age 30, our bodies produce 25 per cent less growth hormone every decade. You can see some results of growth slowdown, like greying hair, expanding waistlines and dry skin. And just like metal fatigue in a ship's steel, some aging signs are less visible: gradual loss of bone density and muscle mass, slower heart rate, weaker eyesight and slower digestion.

Our brains also age and begin to lose nerve cells and show a reduction in volume. Stress, repetitive tasks, and insufficient stimulation further accelerate these deteriorative effects of aging on our minds. Memory and alertness aren't as keen as in younger years. But then there are ways to keep the mind sharp.

WHEN WE LOSE OUR BEARINGS: MIND TROUBLES

The root of all health is in the brain. The trunk of it is in emotion. The branches and leaves are the body. The flower of health blooms when all parts work together.

– Ancient Kurdish proverb

On 24 March 2015 people around the world were shocked to hear that a pilot had intentionally crashed his plane with 149 people on board. Co-pilot Andreas Lubitz locked the captain out of the cockpit and flew Germanwings Flight 9525 directly into the French Alps.

Similar cases have occurred in shipping. For instance, in 1828, Captain Pringle Stokes, who commanded the HMS *Beagle*, shot himself after a round of depression. It was a sad ending for a captain of the famous ship that had carried Charles Darwin on his extraordinary voyages.

Statistics show that over 1,000 seafarers have committed suicide in the last 50 years. This is the most devastating result of a mind-body machine breakdown.

Unfortunately, when we battle stress, confusion, and anxiety, we all suffer poor states of mind. High levels of stress may affect your concentration, alertness, and judgment. An overstressed professional then becomes incapable of handling even moderately challenging tasks. If left unmanaged, this stress can cause heart and body troubles, not to mention the damage it can do to our relationships when we speak words in anger or distress.

Let's face it. Stress is an inescapable part of life, with far-reaching consequences. We can, however, choose how we react to it. If you can tune your mind-body machine to stay relaxed and resilient even in stressful situations, you'll have an unfailing resource to help you fulfil the demands of life. The stresses of life are like the wind and waves at sea. It is up to you to keep your bearings steady on course.

FIVE PRACTICAL STRATEGIES TO KEEP THE MIND-BODY MACHINE IN TOP SHAPE:

1   Eat right
2   Sleep well
3   Exercise
4   Stay positive
5   De-stress.

1 EAT RIGHT, FUEL UP

First we eat, then we do everything else.

– MFK Fisher, author

In 1499, Vasco da Gama was the first European to reach India by sea. In 1519, Magellan's expedition was the first to circumnavigate the globe. Both these famous navigators began their journey with a crew of around 200, but lost around half of them due to scurvy. Scurvy is caused by lack of vitamin C. Something as simple as the lack of a proper and nutritious diet could have jeopardised these commercially and politically important maritime ventures.

Poor eating habits also cause lower energy and higher stress levels while a balanced diet keeps bones, muscles, and the organs healthy. A good leader cannot ignore the value of a wholesome diet.

Eat well, both in quality and in quantity. The Harvard Healthy Eating Plate suggests that 50 per cent of our meal should be vegetables and fruits. The remaining is equally divided between grain and proteins. Ideally, your food plate should have different natural colours, such as green, yellow, and red, which are naturally present on vegetables and grains. Brown bread, rice, and sugar are healthier than their white or polished versions.

Make sure the nutrients in your food are not lost by overcooking. Snack healthy; opt for nuts and sandwiches rather than a packet of crisps. I recommend that ships have 'mess committees' in order to have more inputs regarding the variety and quality of the food on the menu. You can also take food and vitamin supplements as prescribed by your doctor, but these should never be a substitute for a balanced diet.

Eat at regular intervals and at meal times whenever you can. On a ship, meal times are often disturbed if the ship has to enter or leave a port, but ensure you and your team are not working on an empty stomach. Lastly, stay sociable; sitting at the table with your shipmates creates a positive atmosphere and builds goodwill.

Water is as important as food. It is the driving force of nature and makes up about 60 per cent of our body weight. Make sure you drink plenty of it every day. Water carries nutrients to our cells and flushes toxins out of vital organs. Even mild dehydration can drain your energy, make you tired, and may trigger headaches.

I have seen several seafarers suffer from kidney stones. This is a result of long periods of dehydration, especially if they have been working in hot environments. Don't wait to feel thirsty; that is usually a late indicator of your body's need of water. And don't underestimate how much water your body might need. You continuously lose water when you breathe, sweat, and urinate. Therefore, you need regular water intake to stay hydrated.

HEALTHY INTAKE OF FOOD AND WATER ARE THE FUEL FOR THE MIND-BODY MACHINE.

2 SLEEP WELL, BEAT FATIGUE

Fatigue makes fools of us all. It robs you of your skills and your judgment, and it blinds you to creative solutions.

– Harvey Mackay, businessman

The grounding of the container ship *Cita* did not make as many headlines as the *Exxon Valdez* but it was no less dramatic. The navigator had dozed off when the ship crashed onto the Isles of Scilly. He had not rested enough before the watch, and could not help himself from falling asleep. What is worrying is that in a recent survey, one in four seafarers admitted to having fallen asleep while on watch!

Research shows that lack of sleep for over 17 hours can impair mental performance to the same extent as having 0.05 per cent alcohol content in the blood (BAC). Hand-eye coordination, speed of response, risk avoidance, accuracy, attention, and memory deteriorate with reduced sleep. Having a BAC of over 0.05 per cent makes it illegal to drive a car in most countries; how can it be safe to navigate a ship in a similarly debilitating sleep-deprived condition?

Seafarers are required by law to rest at least 10 hours a day. To truly benefit, focus on sleep, and not just rest. Sleep is the body's way to recover and recharge itself for the next day.

Good sleep aids the stable production of the hormones which are essential for maintaining body organs. The long-term effects of poor sleep include hypertension, digestive disorders, and heart disease.

On a ship, shift work, disruptions for port arrivals, ship movement, noise, and vibrations can affect your sleep quality. Eyeshades or sleeping masks, ear-comforters, blackout curtains, and a comfortable mattress help improve sleep quality. A 30-minute nap, when possible, also helps you recharge and wake up to a 'second day'.

Pre-sleep routines can also help you relax. So can reading positive books or watching movies, provided you don't overdo it. Regular exercise also readies the body for sleep.

Things to avoid before sleep time include: eating heavily, taking sleeping pills without consulting a doctor, and alcohol. Once the effect of alcohol wears off, your sleep will most likely get disrupted.

What do you do when you have not slept enough and feel fatigued? The first step is acknowledging that you are tired, and the second is saying so. On one occasion, I was on watch as we departed a tanker terminal. The ship had to pass through congested traffic lanes and several offshore oil platforms. As chief officer, I had been awake for most of the day supervising cargo operations. I didn't feel alert enough to navigate the ship for the next four hours. So, I summoned my courage and discussed this problem with the captain. Thankfully, he was supportive and offered to keep watch while I recharged my batteries. My captain was a great leader; he took care of his team. He was also pleased that I had decided not to let my tiredness affect the safety of the ship.

3 EXERCISE: BECOME A MAN OF STEEL

Lifts are for pregnant women and those who can't walk.

– Mærsk Mc-Kinney Møller

Chairman and CEO of the global shipping giant, AP Moller–Maersk Group, Mærsk Mc-Kinney Møller insisted on climbing the five flights of stairs in his office every day until the age of 98.

If the chief engineer of the *Apollo* had invested more time in exercise, he would have probably made it safely to the top of the ladder.

It takes just 30 minutes a day to stay physically and mentally fit. 'I don't have the time', usually means, 'I don't want to'. Sometimes, though, there really isn't sufficient time, so if yesterday was hectic, make sure you exercise today. Combine a mix of aerobic exercises, strength training, and stretches in your routine.

Cross-trainers are ideal aerobic exercise machines for ships, as you can burn calories even when the ship is rolling, and without straining your joints. Some people prefer multi-function weight machines over free weights as they don't have to worry about a barbell falling on them or pulling a muscle beyond its standard range of motion.

EXERCISE KEEPS THE BODY, MIND, AND CONFIDENCE IN TOP SHAPE.

Back injuries aboard ships often result from underdeveloped or tense muscles. Strengthen your core with abdomen and back exercises. Whatever routine you choose, start with a warm-up and exercise for at least 30 minutes without a break. Finish off with stretches.

Before starting work on deck or in the engine room, stretch your limbs. Being flexible not only protects your back but also increases your power. Anyone who has learnt martial arts will agree that the more flexible you are, the stronger you can land a punch!

Exercise tones and strengthens muscles while also helping you unwind. Research has shown that people with poor physical health are at higher risk of experiencing common mental health problems.

Studies also show that exercise releases certain 'feel-good' chemicals like dopamine, endorphins, and serotonin in our brain. It is thus not surprising that physical activity also brings with it a positive self-image, a sense of alertness, self-confidence, stamina for work, assertiveness, and a boost in mental processes.

4 B POSITIVE

Your mind is a garden,

your thoughts are the seeds.

You can grow flowers, or

you can grow weeds.

– Anonymous

Be positive. Positive people are better leaders. When leaders stay positive they inspire optimism in their team and deliver positive results. This is why I've had this quote on my desk for many years. It helps me maintain a positive outlook under any situation. How can you do the same?

Smile as often as possible. A smile is the simplest leadership tool that can make you feel positive. Smiling tricks your brain into a positive state of mind, and a cheerful attitude helps others feel comfortable around you.

Keep negative thoughts at bay. This is very important, especially in a dynamic environment like shipping. Everything in our work environment is subject to change; our colleagues, the ship's route, or the shore staff we deal with. It's very easy to fall into the trap of complaining about the attitudes and actions of others and to let them affect our mood and thoughts.

YOU CANNOT LEAD A POSITIVE LIFE WITH A NEGATIVE MIND.

Whenever a negative thought enters your mind, gently but firmly push it away. A healthy concern for the safety of the ship is fine. Other than that, worrying, particularly about things outside of your control, won't solve any problems. You simply cannot live a positive life with a negative mind. Condition your mind to stay positive.

Avoid negative conversations. Even when you get frustrated or disappointed, remember that talking negatively about a person, an organisation, or a situation never solves problems. It only erodes your leadership value in the eyes of anyone who is listening.

Attract inspiring and positive thoughts. Read inspirational or spiritual books. Compliment others for work well done. Research has found that people with deep spiritual or religious involvement have better mental health and are more effective leaders. They have better self-control, self-esteem, and confidence, and they can weather stress better than most.

Meditate. Allow at least 10 minutes a day to empty your mind of all thoughts. Meditation relaxes your mind. It also allows your subconscious to work in tandem with your conscious mind. In this way your conscious mind picks up helpful insights from your subconscious. Research has also proven that meditation lowers the risk of heart attacks.

Socialise. Be there for your shipmates. Studies show that people who offer support to one another can cope well with stress. People with a sense of humour are usually perceived as positive individuals and as better leaders. Laugh more; laughter is a great tonic, containing B positive.

5 DE-STRESS: HAVE A RELIEF VALVE

It's not stress that kills us; it is our reaction to it.

– Hans Selye, pioneering endocrinologist

Captain Pastrengo Rugiati had spent 15 years in command with a clean record, but fell victim to unmanaged stress. The captain of the 120,000-tonne tanker *Torrey Canyon* was bothered by several issues; his wife had been ill for some time, he was overdue for relief, and his relationship with the chief officer was strained. To add to his list of worries, he had just received a message from the port agent that if he missed the tide, his ship would have to wait for another week off the port of Milford Haven in the United Kingdom. Also, Captain Rugiati was concerned about keeping the ship on an even keel, to give a good appearance when entering port. All these unresolved issues compounded his stress to a point where his ability to make rational judgments was compromised.

Feeling under pressure, the captain then made a series of errors. He disregarded his chief officer's course correction and decided to make an unplanned passage through the Isles of Scilly. In trying to manage all the issues bothering him, Captain Rugiati's mind began to wander; he failed to notice that the rudder was still on autopilot. This meant that his manual steering orders had no effect. By the time he realised his mistake, the *Torrey Canyon* was already upon the rocks off the Isles of Scilly. The pollution from the grounding was so severe that despite attempts by the Royal Air Force to burn the oil by bombing the wreck, the remaining oil affected many shores of northern Europe.

The modern workplace can generate an indefinite supply of stress. A survey indicated that 66 per cent of people who suffer from stress-related health issues believed that their workplace was responsible for it. In a mariner's environment, tight schedules, work overload, lack of sleep, lack of entertainment and social interaction, relationships with colleagues and family, and health issues can all lead to stress. Ship motion, vibration and noise, smells of oil, paint and grease, heat in the engine room, and wind chill factor on deck compound the stress in an already demanding job.

LEARNING TO RELIEVE STRESS EVERY DAY IS KEY TO A HAPPY CAREER.

Now, some of the stress we experience is self-inflicted. Pending work, delayed decisions, and lack of planning increase stress. Stress leads to emotions such as anger, resentment, frustration, indifference, sadness, and a feeling of being overwhelmed or inadequate. Physical symptoms of stress include lack of appetite, disturbed sleep, frequent headaches, tightness of the neck, unease of stomach, and tightness in the chest.

If not released daily, stress accumulates and manifests in the form of poor concentration, interpersonal conflicts, poor decision-making, and mistakes. Worse still, if unmanaged over time, it can lead to depression, hypertension, and heart disease.

The first step to dealing with stress is to accept that stress is a *normal* part of our daily life. Next is to learn to manage it in a way that does not affect your leadership abilities, and even prevent it from building up. In order to do this, you must have a stress relief valve, just like a boiler has a relief valve to let off excess steam. Keep the mind-body machine active through good diet, sleep, and exercise. Positive mindsets and habits, and routines such as meditation and socialising are all strong stress repellents.

You owe it to yourself and your shipmates to keep your mind-body machine in top shape, stress free, and ready for action. A well-maintained mind-body machine is crucial to building and supporting your leadership day after day.

THE MACHINE OF A LEADER

- You are only as good as your mind-body. Take care of it!
- Mind-body disciplines include (a) healthy diet; (b) sound sleep; (c) stimulating exercise; (d) positive thinking; and (e) relieving stress.
- Just like a ship's engine, your mind-body machine has to run every day.

LEADING YOURSELF - THE STEERING MODEL ©

How do you steer your own course through the wind and waves of life? Use this steering model as an aid-to-memory, to lead yourself.

Lead your Motivation
1. Self-Confidence
2. Inspiration
3. Body over Mind
4. Own your Goals
5. Conquer Demotivation

The Steering Model

Lead your Attention
1. Give yourself Time
2. Prepare to be Distracted
3. Stay Mindfully Manual
4. Engage your Senses
5. Focus your Vision

Lead your Habits
1. Planning
2. Time Management
3. Organization

Lead your Mind-Body Machine
1. Eat Well
2. Sleep Well
3. Exercise
4. Stay Positive
5. Destress

13

TEAM: ALL HANDS ON DECK

No member of a crew is praised for the rugged individuality of his rowing.

– Ralph Waldo Emerson, poet

MY FIRST LESSON IN TEAMWORK was in a lifeboat.

Lifeboats provide a means of escape in case a ship is in danger of sinking. Regulations require that these boats be tested in water every few months to ensure that the crew is ready for emergencies. We were at anchor off Kandla on the west coast of India, and the captain decided to test the lifeboat. He assigned the junior officers and us cadets to the task.

We lowered the boat to water, unhooked it from the ship's winch, started the engines, and made a test run around the ship. We were excited with this change in routine, so we used this opportunity to take some pictures of the ship as well. As we headed back to be hauled up, we were in for a surprise: the boat's engines died. To make matters worse, the strong currents in the anchorage started pushing us away from the ship and out to sea.

The third officer decided we should start rowing. Easier said than done! The oars were of solid wood, about 15 feet long, and weighed close to 10 kilograms each. Oars on modern lifeboats are just for a back-up in case the engines fail, so we had last rowed during our training in the academy two years ago and our skills were rusty. We were rowing, but the boat wasn't moving ahead. Instead, it swayed from side to side as the six of us rowed at a different rhythm. Then, we quickly started drifting further away from the ship. It would be dark in a few hours, and we could be lost at sea if we didn't do something different, fast.

I grew up on an island, and I know a bit about how boats are rowed. I suggested that our senior officer should pace the rowers.

The team agreed that we all dip our oars on his shout of 'Down', and recover on the call of 'Up'. After a few attempts, we were finally moving our oars in a consistent rhythm. New life surged through the boat as we rowed as a team, and the boat finally started moving forward. The captain had prepared the other lifeboat to rescue us, but now he and the rest of the crew cheered us on as we came closer to the ship. It was as though we were performing at the Olympics – the Olympics of Life.

We finally made it to the ship, just by rowing. The crew gave us a cheerful welcome and the captain let us know that he was proud of our team effort. So were we!

We learned some important lessons in teamwork that day:

Each of us had to do our part to bring the boat back. The ship operates 24 hours a day; there are machineries to run, ropes to tend, and watches to keep. One person can't be responsible for it all; you need all hands on deck. Some are leaders and some are subordinates, but regardless of the number of stripes, everyone is a team member and each plays an equally important role.

Leaders are decisive and lead from the front at all times, especially during a crisis. Our officer at the helm immediately decided to row once the engines failed; he directed the boat towards the ship, and provided the rhythm for the rowers. Every team needs a leader to direct and coordinate. Others need to follow the rhythm and pace that he thus sets.

Leaders influence and energise their team towards their goals. That same officer made us believe that we could reach the ship in spite of the strong opposing current. Had we not rowed together, the officer would have failed to bring the boat back to the ship. He needed the coordinated efforts of his team to succeed.

The officer put aside his ego. He was open enough to listen to my suggestion, and his acknowledgement created an atmosphere of trust. Trust in one another is important, whether it is in rowing a boat or completing a project on time.

Good communication. This is imperative for successful teamwork. The leader's shouts of "Up" and "Down" ensured that the team rowed as one. This is how good communication coordinated our efforts to make us one strong and cohesive unit.

EACH OF US IS A LINK IN THE CHAIN

The strength of the team is each member. The strength of each member is the team.

– Phil Jackson, basketball coach

A chain is only as strong its weakest link. On the boat, we could row only as fast as the slowest person. On a ship, you're only as effective as your team allows you to be.

The crew that comes on board is usually competent and well trained. But how we come together and work as an efficient unit is entirely up to us. Our careers and lives depend on it. One navigator making a wrong manoeuvre can cause a collision. An engineer who overlooks an alarm allows a generator breakdown. A carelessly disposed cigarette may start a raging fire in the accommodation. A seaman failing to close a ventilator during a fire compromises the extinguishing efforts. A cook unable to prepare good food lowers the morale of the ship. You may have the expertise and motivation to perform your job well, but how do you ensure your team performs equally well?

The objective of teamwork is to make every link in the proverbial chain strong, fit properly with one another, pull in the same direction and together, achieve more.

Poor coordination leads to confusion and counterproductive activity. A case in point is the flooding of the bulk carrier *Great Majesty*. The ship was discharging manganese ore at Port Kembla, Australia. The Chinese chief engineer instructed the No. 2 ballast pump to be opened for maintenance. He also instructed the Bangladeshi chief officer not to operate this pump.

The chief officer understood that the pump was not to be operated but was unsure if the ballast tanks could be filled naturally, by gravity. He did not confirm his view with the chief engineer. Instead, he simply assumed there was no risk in ballasting the tanks, bypassing the pumps. The chief officer opened a valve in the adjacent ballast line. The sea intake was not isolated; this meant that as soon as the ballast line valve was opened, water rapidly filled the engine room through the open pump. By the time anyone realised the mistake, sea water had damaged 22 electric motors and shorted the power supply to the ship.

As a team member, you have to deal with different personalities, diverse backgrounds and communication styles even as you face the daily challenges at sea.

Ships are unique workplaces. Team members turn over every month, if not every week. This means seafarers have to quickly integrate within the team and build trust with one another. If this does not happen, people may hesitate to communicate with each other, as it happened on the *Great Majesty*. If the team is not bound by trust, it can come apart at the first sign of stress. Thankfully, you can improve your teamwork skills with practice.

PULLING TOGETHER AS A CHAIN: A GREAT TEAM

A single arrow is easily broken, but not ten in a bundle.

– Japanese proverb

Many years after the lifeboat incident, I was rewarded with another great display of teamwork. On New Year's Eve, 2004, I was in command and we were sailing into the Black Sea from the Bosporus Strait, scheduled to enter Constanţa, Romania, early the next morning. We had agreed as a team to postpone the New Year's Eve celebrations, so we could rest before our hectic day in port.

Thirty minutes to midnight, we were awoken abruptly by a fire alarm. The washing machine in the ship's laundry had short-circuited and caught fire. As smoke filled up one of the passageways, our team swung into action. I rushed to my position on the bridge to coordinate the entire emergency response. The chief officer took charge of the firefighters, the chief engineer ensured that the water hoses were charged, and the support team choked the oxygen to the fire by shutting off ventilation. The effort was precise and efficient; we would later find out that the fire was put out in under two minutes!

Twenty-two men, most of whom were asleep when danger struck, had come together at this crucial moment when it was needed most. The efforts we had put into building our team over the last few weeks were evident in the way we effectively resolved the crisis. The outcome defined great teamwork for me.

Research affirms that the quality of our relationships with our colleagues also determines our happiness at work. From the time we were nearly stranded on the lifeboat to the time we fought the fire, and even to this day, I know without a doubt that I need the help of my team to succeed in times of trouble.

A Golden Stripes mariner can achieve his maximum potential not just by working alone, but when he is able to tap into the energy of his team. Great teams don't form by themselves; they require patience, consistent effort, and a few simple strategies.

T.E.A.M. (TOGETHER EVERYONE ACHIEVES MORE)

- A Golden Stripes mariner is one who works well with his team.

- A team needs a leader, and a leader needs his team to succeed.

- Teamwork requires communication, consistent effort, and a common direction to achieve its goals.

14

ADD VALUE TO YOUR TEAM: TURBOCHARGE

Engineers ... are not superhuman. They make mistakes in
their assumptions, in their calculations, in their conclusions.
That they make mistakes is forgivable; that they catch them is
imperative. Thus it is the essence of modern engineering not
only to be able to check one's own work but also to have one's
work checked and to be able to check the work of others.

– Henry Petroski, *To Engineer Is Human:*
The Role of Failure in Successful Design

THE BULK CARRIER *HANJIN BOMBAY* was departing from the
port of Tauranga, New Zealand, loaded with a full cargo of logs for
Kunsan, South Korea. Nothing about the day was unusual, that is until
they started increasing speed. A malfunctioning valve in the engine
cooling system caused the engine cooling water to rise above the
normal temperature.

A strange thing about automation is that it does only what it is
programmed to do. The engine safety control system activated when
the temperature of the cooling water was too high. It automatically
slowed and shut down the engine to prevent it becoming permanently
damaged.

Unfortunately, at that time, the ship was still negotiating a tricky
turn in the outbound channel. There was no time for the bridge team
to respond to this sudden engine stoppage. There was neither time
to deploy the anchors nor to manoeuvre the ship to a safer area. The
navigators lost control of the ship and it ran aground on the eastern
shore of the channel.

The valve malfunction was unexpected. Still, smart engineering
and teamwork could have prevented the ship from grounding. Had the
engine room team alerted the bridge when the problem first appeared,
tugs could have been requested to control the movement of the ship.

Had the engineers used the override for the automatic shutdown just for a little while, the ship could have made it past the narrow channel. They did make an effort, but it was not effective enough for their team. Instead of focusing only on resolving the cooling-water issue, had they thought of the larger consequences for the ship, the outcome would have been different.

Each of us has to perform to our best to add value to our team. When we fail, our team suffers. While our job responsibility is important, our role as a member of the team is much greater. Like the cylinders in an engine, we have to work to our best, and in perfect rhythm with our team.

What does a great team member look like? Like you or me! We are both leaders and followers at the same time, and our roles are interchangeable. A chief engineer is the head of the engine room team, and at the same time he supports the navigators' needs. He also has to support the ship manager's maintenance plans. Only when individuals in a team, from ship-owner right down to oiler, work towards a common goal and inspire each other, can you build a successful team.

If you want to be part of a great team, start with yourself. Instead of wishing for others to be better team players, *your* actions can turbocharge and inspire great teamwork.

FIVE EASY STEPS THAT CAN HELP YOU BECOME THE IDEAL SHIPMATE THAT YOU ALSO WANT OTHERS TO BE:

1 Own your deck
2 Put your ship first
3 Look out for your mates
4 Take the initiative
5 Be an effective follower.

1 OWN YOUR DECK

Individual commitment to a group effort – that is what makes a team work, a company work, a society work, a civilization work.

– Vince Lombardi, American football coach

The chief officer on the general cargo ship *Danio* dozed off while on navigation watch. He had been asleep for about three hours when the ship grounded at full speed in the Farne Islands nature reserve off the east coast of England. All the while, the remaining crew of six had entrusted their safety to the hands of their shipmate. One person's mistake can result in disaster for the whole team, so take your responsibility seriously.

IT'S YOUR SHIP; IF YOU CARE FOR IT, IT WILL CARE FOR YOU.

Every seafarer is expected to perform his duty to his best, without being asked to do so. Doing your best means using the fullest of your professional expertise, attention, and diligence. Pay attention to detail. Check your own work as if there is no one else to do it.

Take ownership of your area of work. Think of the ship as your own. Be a star performer in your area of responsibility. Be a champion for relevant policies and procedures.

You many not receive a pat on your back every time you do a good job. Superiors are often quite preoccupied with their own work and it may seem as though they don't notice. The truth is, although people appreciate the work you do they do not always say so aloud. Regardless, you must own your deck and serve your ship.

2 PUT YOUR SHIP FIRST

A boat doesn't go forward if each one is rowing their own way.

– Swahili proverb

In 1993, the tanker *Braer* spilt 84,700 tonnes of crude oil into the sea after it foundered off the Shetland Islands. Around 83 million US dollars were paid in claims. The salmon farms along the Shetland Islands' coast were destroyed by the oil spill, resulting in another loss of 25 million US dollars. Good seamanship, as well as a 'putting the ship first' mindset, could have prevented this accident.

The ship was carrying spare steel pipes on its upper deck to be used for repairs on its voyage from Norway to Canada. Unfortunately, these pipes had not been properly secured. The pipes came loose when the ship moved boisterously in gale force seas. Once unrestrained, the pipes struck and damaged the air vents adjacent to the fuel tanks. With waves splashing onto the deck at the same time, sea-water soon entered the fuel tanks through the damaged air vents.

The sea water which had entered the tanks contaminated the fuel for the generators and the main engine of the ship. The engines

ADD VALUE TO YOUR TEAM: TURBOCHARGE

stopped, and the *Braer* lost power. Within hours, the ship drifted helplessly onto the rocks.

The captain and the navigators hadn't put the ship first during that voyage. Since the chief engineer was responsible for securing the pipes, the captain and other navigators left him to it and didn't step outside the comfort of the wheelhouse to check the conditions on deck. It was as if they had adopted a 'don't know, don't care' approach.

Even after the pipes had broken loose, the captain left it to the chief engineer and chief officer to control the situation. He didn't turn the vessel to a heading which could have allowed the crew to either secure or jettison the pipes. Nor did he offer any support to the chief engineer when water in the fuel was discovered.

Ultimately, they all lost the ship.

Often we get so engrossed with our roles, our departments, and our targets that we drift away from our colleagues. We lose sight of what is best for our team and our ship. We fail to recognise the connection between our shipmate's success and our safety.

If you don't care about your shipmate's problem, he may not help you when you need help. If you remain focused only on your work, and not on what your team requires, communication weakens. Instead, we end up playing favourites, or we criticise and withhold information or help from a colleague who is struggling with his workload. The problem aggravates when our shipmates are from different backgrounds. Unresolved personal conflicts eventually erupt and erode trust within a team.

Your leadership hinges on your ability to work professionally in a team in spite of differences in opinions, backgrounds, or working styles. Putting your ship first means being adaptable and going beyond your job description when required, for instance, when workloads peak or when a colleague is sick.

Resolve difference of opinions in an objective and empathetic way. Put yourself in the other person's shoes. When in conflict, a win-lose result may provide momentary satisfaction, but in the long run, a win-win outcome helps both the leader and his team. Putting the team's interests ahead of your own is the only way for your team to succeed.

3 LOOK OUT FOR YOUR MATES

Be shipmates that watch out for each other. You are some of our best warning systems in existence. You are intrusive leaders. That is the key of taking care of one another.

– Vice Admiral Matthew L Nathan, US Navy

Parani's Porthole Model of Expertise ©

Parani's Porthole Model of Expertise ©

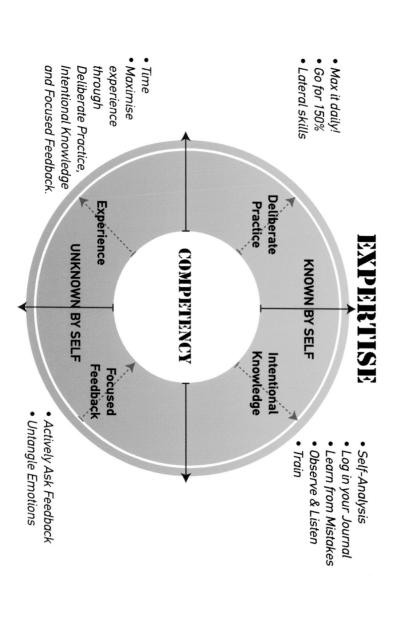

EXPERTISE

- Max it daily!
- Go for 150%
- Lateral skills

- Time
- Maximise experience through Deliberate Practice, Intentional Knowledge and Focused Feedback.

- Self-Analysis
- Log in your Journal
- Learn from Mistakes
- Observe & Listen
- Train

- Actively Ask Feedback
- Untangle Emotions

COMPETENCY

KNOWN BY SELF

UNKNOWN BY SELF

- Deliberate Practice
- Intentional Knowledge
- Experience
- Focused Feedback

The Steering Model

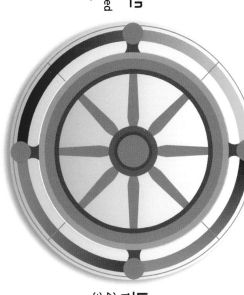

Lead your Attention
1. Give yourself Time
2. Prepare to be Distracted
3. Stay Mindfully Manual
4. Engage your Senses
5. Focus your Vision

Lead your Motivation
1. Self-Confidence
2. Inspiration
3. Body over Mind
4. Own your Goals
5. Conquer Demotivation

Lead your Mind-Body Machine
1. Eat Well
2. Sleep Well
3. Exercise
4. Stay Positive
5. Destress

Lead your Habits
1. Planning
2. Time Management
3. Organization

The Flange Model

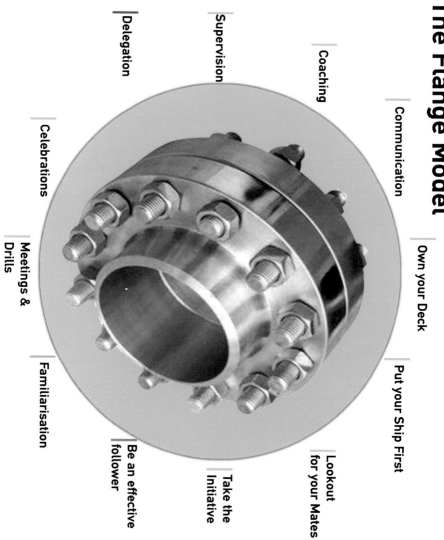

- Communication
- Coaching
- Supervision
- Delegation
- Celebrations
- Meetings & Drills
- Familiarisation
- Be an effective follower
- Take the Initiative
- Lookout for your Mates
- Put your Ship First
- Own your Deck

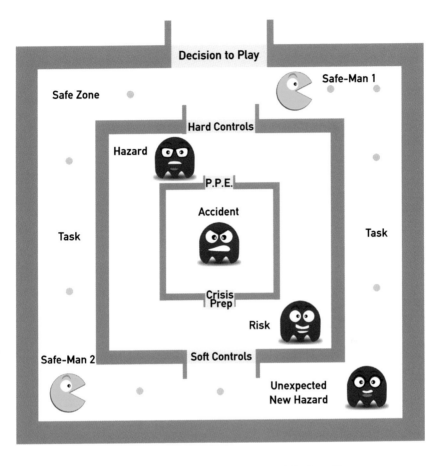

The Safe-Man Game Model of Safety ©

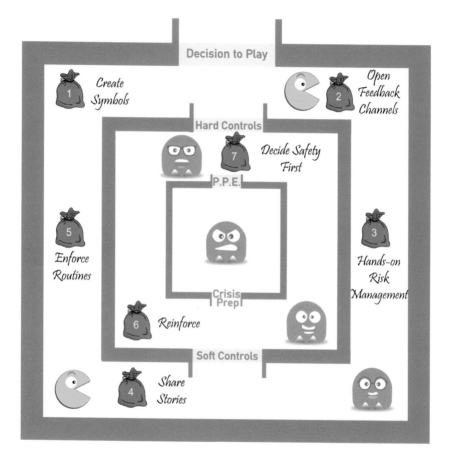

Safety Culture – The Energy for the Game ©

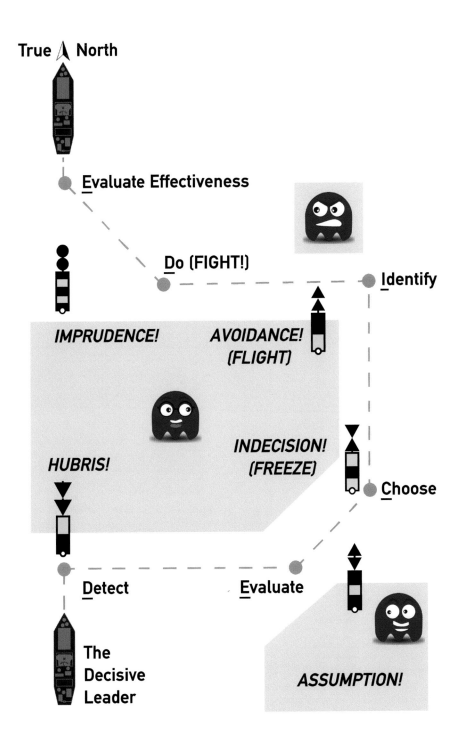

True **^** North

Evaluate Effectiveness

Do (FIGHT!)

Identify

IMPRUDENCE!

AVOIDANCE!
(FLIGHT)

HUBRIS!

INDECISION!
(FREEZE)

Choose

Detect

Evaluate

The
Decisive
Leader

ASSUMPTION!

The Decision Making Mnemonic ©

Leader-ship

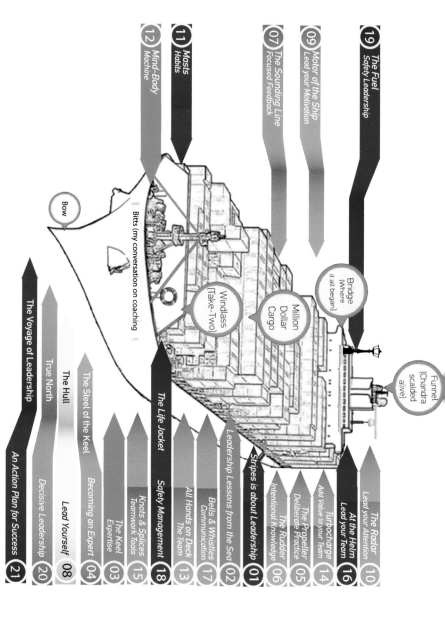

19 The Fuel
Safety Leadership

09 Motor of the Ship
Lead your Motivation

07 The Sounding Line
Focused Feedback

11 Masts
Habits

12 Mind-Body
Machine

Bow

Bitts (my conversation on coaching)

Windlass
(Take-Two)

Million
Dollar
Cargo

Bridge
(Where
it all began)

Funnel
(Chandra
scalded
alive)

The Voyage of Leadership

Decisive Leadership 20

True North

The Hull

Lead Yourself 08

The Steel of the Keel

Becoming an Expert 04

The Keel
Expertise

Knots & Splices
Teamwork Tools 15

The Life Jacket

Safety Management 18

All Hands on Deck
The Team 13

Bells & Whistles
Communication 17

Leadership Lessons from the Sea 02

Stripes is about Leadership 01

Intentional Knowledge 06
The Rudder

Deliberate Practice 05
The Propeller

Add Value to your Team 14
Turbocharge

At the Helm
Lead your Team 16

The Radar
Lead your Attention 10

An Action Plan for Success 21

Sergey Gaponov was just 40 years old when he was pulled down by a mooring rope from the deck of his ship and into the water. The Russian deckhand on the *Sea Melody* had not noticed when he stepped into the noose-like bight of a mooring rope. If his fellow crew members had kept an eye out for him, he would probably have survived.

Good team players motivate, guide, mentor, help, and back each other up. When the captain overlooks a course correction during a manoeuvre, the assisting officer should alert him. When the second engineer is struggling to cope with engine maintenance, the chief officer can lend a hand for non-technical tasks. If we don't look out for each other, who else will?

I always recommend the Buddy System on ships, which simply means: work in pairs, look out for each other and alert each other if you see danger. This strategy works exceedingly well in eliminating one-man errors and in reducing accidents.

When newly promoted or when in unfamiliar situations such as new trading areas, new equipment, or a new type of cargo, officers need help from their more experienced colleagues. It's easy to fall into the trap of complaining about the other person's inexperience. Instead, why not reach out to help them?

As a leader, it is your duty and privilege to look out for your team.

4 TAKE THE INITIATIVE: THROW THE LINE

There is a tide in the affairs of men, which taken at the flood, leads on to fortune.

– William Shakespeare, poet and playwright.
Among his many works is *The Tempest*, a play involving a shipwreck

After long voyages, when ships finally arrive in port, they usually have one stinking problem; piled-up garbage from the kitchens and cleaning. With the exception of food waste, regulations do not allow the disposal of garbage at sea. However, waste collected over weeks needs to be disposed of, which in some ports can be quite expensive.

One of our chief officers, Joseph, took the initiative and came up with a simple yet brilliant suggestion. Why not supply the ships with garbage compactors and grinders? The ship was not fitted with this equipment and it would have to be retrofitted. Joseph even prepared a cost–benefit analysis to present to the senior management. We tested the equipment on one of the ships, and the crew were delighted. The compactors reduced the garbage storage space by one-third, and the grinders ensured that more food waste could be disposed at sea. Overall garbage disposal costs at ports went down. So did the stink!

Eventually, the idea was implemented across the fleet, and the investment in additional equipment was recovered in less than two years. But this initiative from Joseph inspired more ideas from others for making our operations even more efficient. People shared best practices across the organisation, which in turn helped us reach a stage of maturity where we were able to get our environmental management system certified to an advanced international standard.

Joseph's initiative made a difference not just to his ship but to the entire fleet. Over the last decade, the momentum created from his initiative has saved the organisation millions of dollars, and it has helped establish a culture of corporate social responsibility. He is a shining example of how one person's initiative can rope in the entire team together. Initiatives fires up the team spirit to do something extraordinary.

Don't just wait to be told to do a job. Get into the habit of volunteering and taking the initiative. Initiative is doing the right thing without being asked to do it, or before it becomes urgent. If you spot areas that need improvement, inform your colleagues and devise a plan to get things done. You will have some extra work following it up, but it will get you into the habit of taking initiative.

Initiative is positive attitude in action. It is the secret sauce that determines success in preventive maintenance, risk management, housekeeping, communication, and in your role as a team member.

As you take more initiative in team activities, be it drills, safety meetings, or even barbecues, your enthusiasm and positive attitude will catch on and inspire your team to do the same.

Active participation in any task improves self-confidence. Seafarers who show interest in areas outside of their own usually gain much more in the long run. So as you take more initiative, you open your mind to learning through action.

By the way, Joseph is now a very successful captain of large ocean-going ships. He is still actively involved in researching new initiatives for fuel savings and reduction of carbon emissions.

5 BE AN EFFECTIVE FOLLOWER: BE THE SUPPORTING FRAME

Followers who tell the truth, and leaders who listen to it, are an unbeatable combination.

– Warren Bennis, management expert

'The junior ranking officer failed to alert the captain about the imminent danger. He assumed that his senior was already aware of the situation and did not need his advice.' This statement holds true for many shipping casualties, such as the one involving the *Axel Spirit* off New York.[10]

Structural frames are usually hidden from view, but they play a vital role in keeping the ship afloat. Similarly, a good follower intentionally supports his leaders to lead well. The problem is that even though we want to help, we often do not know how to.

Good followers know that everyone, including their seniors, can make mistakes. They make the effort to express their professional opinions freely and politely so as to prevent one-man errors. Being a good follower is not the equivalent of being a yes man, or an apple-polisher. What it truly means is that you have faith in your own capabilities, while offering an honest opinion on any situation.

There are three layers of leadership when interacting with your team: (i) leading with discipline, (ii) leading subordinates by example, and (iii) leading superiors with feedback.

To be a good leader, you first need to learn how to follow.

Don't lie, don't bullshit. This was one of the first lessons I learnt in my early seafaring years. Whether it was reporting a problem, preparing maintenance reports, or updating statuses, we learned to report things as soon as they occurred, and not misrepresent or tone down the status. A problem is not necessarily your mistake, but it becomes one when you don't report it. Professional integrity takes years to build – don't lose yours over 'one little lie'.

DON'T LIE, DON'T BULLSHIT.

When your team is working to achieve a common goal, there is pressure on everyone to deliver. You may get yelled at, you may get pushed hard by your seniors, or you may even be rebuked for mistakes; this is the harsh reality in any work environment, particularly high-stress workplaces like a ship. Don't take it personally; resist the urge to say or do something that you may regret later. If the request is a valid one, follow it. Remember this: more is being asked of you for the benefit of your ship and your team, and you are being asked to do it because they know you can deliver more.

Being able to follow orders is also vital in emergencies. In such situations, there's usually no time for discussion and everyone must follow their prescribed duties, no matter what their opinions are.

Being a follower is a responsibility we cannot escape, so it's best to learn how to be an effective follower. After all, you can't ask others to follow you unless you've already proven you know how to follow.

TURBOCHARGE YOUR TEAM

- Good teamwork starts with you.

- You can build a successful team by:

  1 owning your deck and playing your part with a smile

  2 putting your ship first

  3 watching out for others

  4 taking the initiative

  5 being an effective follower.

- Avoid the 'don't know, don't care' approach.

- You become a good team player by being genuinely interested in the welfare of your team.

- Help each other succeed, and think beyond yourself.

15

TEAMWORK TOOLS: KNOTS AND SPLICES

Coming together is a beginning. Keeping together is progress.
Working together is success.

– Henry Ford, founder of the Ford Motor Company. Before this, he was
chief engineer with the Edison Illuminating Company
where he made his own gasoline-powered quadricycle

KNOTS AND SPLICES tie different pieces of rope together. And
how do you bring together different people to form a team? Good
teamwork does not happen by itself, but it is formed with intentional
effort, just as purposefully as we splice ropes together.

I learnt some of the knots and other tools of teamwork the hard
way. I was chief officer of an old bulker that had just been bought by
the ship owners. Our team was new to this ship. We hadn't ever worked
with each other before. The crew were from different backgrounds; on
any given day, there would be at least ten different languages being
spoken at the dinner table. Following an inspection, we were shocked
when the port state control officer handed us a long list of deficiencies.
I thought we had worked very hard to bring the ship up to standard.
But the deficiencies revealed that we clearly hadn't done enough.

After we had fixed the defects and set sail, we sat down to analyse
the report and figure out why we hadn't passed inspection on the first
try. We were terribly disappointed by the poor results, particularly
after having put so much effort into upgrading the ship. The captain
read out the report:

(i) Several hatch cover resting pads with excessive clearance.

As chief officer, this item fell directly under my area of control.
The captain questioned me about it. But while I naturally took the
responsibility for it, I had in fact relied on the bosun to let me know
if he found any defects on deck. Later, I searched for answers with the

bosun; he said, 'I thought I fixed it all right, I didn't know we had to check the clearances.'

(ii) Oil in the bow thruster room bilges.

This I had observed earlier, but I assumed that the first engineer would take care of it as this fell under the 'machinery space' domain. He had an assumption of his own: that I would take care of it because these bilges were outside the engine room and therefore, were 'deck space'. The captain admitted that he too was at fault because he had failed to notice it; he hadn't examined the room closely because it wasn't part of his 'usual' route on deck rounds.

(iii) Oily rags not stowed properly.

The third engineer put his hands up in exasperation and said, 'I asked everyone to put the rags in the special drums but it looks like everyone forgot my instructions.'

(iv) During the fire drill, not all the ventilators for the galley were shut.

We all agreed that we had not practised the drills realistically. We were too busy sorting out operational issues after the takeover of the bulker. As a result, we hadn't been sufficiently focused during drills. Among other things, we hadn't practised shutting off the air supply during the drills, and so when the inspector asked us to respond to a fire in the kitchen, we skipped some critical steps.

(v) Some fire hoses were leaking.

This time, we all turned to look at the third officer, but his reason was understandable: 'I had to check both lifeboats, 47 fire extinguishers, and 36 fire hoses. I had to test each of the hoses and repair them one by one. I simply hadn't gotten around to the ones that were defective. I was overworked and overloaded.'

It was a disappointing start. The inspection and report exposed the fact that we had not yet implemented the safety management system on board, and that we were all ill-prepared for an emergency.

So, what next? We were to have a repeat inspection in 30 days, when we returned to the same port. In the meantime, the ship's superintendent joined us and offered some useful advice:

'The problem isn't with the ship. It's with your teamwork. You need to be focused, and as a team you need better coordination, communication and motivation.'

Team building on a ship is quite different from any other

environment. There's a new person on the team every few weeks, most likely from a different background and at a different experience level. So how do you transform a group of people on a ship into an effective team, as quickly as possible? There's no human resources department on board to help with team bonding. And even if there was one, each member of the team is still responsible for, and expected to contribute to, building the team.

IMPLEMENT THESE FOUR TEAM-BUILDING TOOLS:

1   Familiarisation
2   Meetings
3   Drills
4   Celebrations.

1 FAMILIARISE: KNOW YOUR ROPES

On her deck, sailors moved fast and knowingly back and forth. Of course, the crew of a dozen was not big, but you can see that the seafarers were skilled and running the ship easily, as if they were playing games in spite of waves and winds. With such skill and knowledge of the sea, they would have been extremely dangerous if they had in mind something as insidious as robbery.

– Yury Vasiliev, *Over the Equator, Pages from the Journal of Russian Trailblazer Philip Efremov*

Familiarising oneself with the ship and with each other enables team members to feel comfortable enough to quickly settle into the ship. People always feel more at ease after they've familiarised themselves with their routines and started integrating with the rest of the team.

On the old bulker, this had not happened. I had not made the bosun familiar with the inspection procedures for the hatch cover resting pads, causing us to fail this portion of the inspection. Injuries, machinery damages, and navigation accidents sometimes occur because the crew isn't yet familiar with operating and maintaining the equipment.

Familiarisation matters. The United States National Transportation Safety Board found that when the airplane cockpit crew was new, there was a 73 per cent chance of an incident on the first day. I have observed over the course of my career that a similar percentage of navigational errors occur within the first two weeks of a change in the ship's command.

When crew members are familiarised with their tasks, they know their respective duties and how to contribute to the team. They fully understand the risks involved with a task, and can be trusted to keep themselves and their shipmates safe. The process of familiarisation encourages new colleagues to open up to each other and establish effective channels of communication.

2 MEETINGS: MAKE THE LOOP

Meetings are at the heart of an effective organisation, and each meeting is an opportunity to clarify issues, set new directions, sharpen focus, create alignment, and move objectives forward.

– Paul Axtell, author, *Meetings Matter*

At least three deficiencies in the port state control inspection could have been prevented if we had held regular meetings on board. If I and the first engineer had met and talked about who would be responsible to maintain the bow-thruster compartment, the confusion would have been sorted out earlier. Reminding everyone during general meetings that oily rags need to go in the colour-coded drums would have helped to improve compliance with procedures.

Had we met before the inspection, all of us would have been aware of the third officer's pending maintenance on the fire hoses. We could have then assigned more people to lend him a hand with the fire hoses.

Set up meetings regularly and not just when you're having problems. It always amazes me how many problems come to light during such meetings. While it is very tempting to put off meetings under the pretext of being very busy, my experience has taught me that these meetings are crucial and should not be cancelled unless there's a pressing reason to do so.

MEETINGS ARE WHERE TEAM FOCUS IS ACHIEVED.

Not everyone loves meetings, especially those of us who are more introverted. If you're among the quiet types, here's how to make your meetings as productive and painless as possible:

- Cap them at 30 minutes.

- Always announce the agenda at the outset. It helps people to prepare and set expectations. A template helps to get the meeting off to a quick start and in the required direction. When you structure your meeting, the entire crew will appreciate your taking their valuable time into consideration.

- Set an amiable atmosphere. Start and finish on time, sit or stand in circles. Offer snacks and drinks as appropriate.

- Take notes to record comments and draft an action plan.

- Encourage participation. Meetings are not the place to display authority, order, shout, argue, or preach. Sure, there will always be teammates who like to talk a lot or dominate conversations. But when someone begins to drift to irrelevant points, remind them that the meeting has to end on time. Bring the topic back on track or move on to the next subject. And remember: humour can help diffuse any tension and move the meeting along productively.

- Conclude. Discussions are great teamwork tools, but they must always end in action plans. The last two minutes of the meeting should be spent summarising who will do what, by when, and how you will communicate.

For training or safety meetings, I recommend using short topical videos or case studies, to get the discussion started. Allow everyone to speak without interruption. Draw out reluctant speakers by asking them open-ended questions such as:

'What would you do in such a situation?'

'What unsafe situations did you observe on deck this week?'

Briefings on a ship are meetings of a shorter duration. They're about 10 minutes long, just before the start of the day, of a manoeuvre, or an overhaul. They help deliver last-minute reminders as well as create the right frame of mind before the crew begin their work.

Motivate and energise. Have you noticed players emerge from a team huddle before a basketball game? They do this to pump each other up, and enter the court with renewed focus and energy. It is no different on your ship. After your team huddle, strive to end your meetings on a positive note and with a clear plan of action. When you meet and conclude with purpose, your team feels the combined force which motivates each person to want to do his part for the team to succeed.

I've always found meetings to be a good way to connect with and motivate my team. Meetings provide face to face time, which makes us comfortable communicating with each other. Getting an opportunity to speak also helps team members build self-confidence. In addition, regular meetings help assess people's individual capabilities, which is very important for a leader to know.

3 DRILLS: FLEX THE TEAM MUSCLE

Remember: upon the conduct of each depends the fate of all.

– Alexander III of Macedon (Alexander the Great)

During the port state control inspection, our team had failed to stop the air supply to an imaginary fire. If the fire was real, we would have surely lost the battle to contain it.

When you train together during drills, you develop the 'team muscle' – that special element of strength and coordination in a team that can overcome any situation. Like any muscle in your body, the more you flex your team's muscle, the easier it is to work as a team.

Drills are teamwork theories put in action. As we carry them out, we observe each person's capabilities. We're forced to back each other up. We understand best how to communicate with each other.

Drills can also be fun! They boost motivation, help break the monotony of daily routines, and give the crew confidence that they can tackle any situation. For one security drill, I secretly asked the electrical engineer to hide in the crane cabin and called for a stowaway search. You can imagine the fun everyone had teasing the electrical engineer when the 'stowaway' was caught!

4 CELEBRATE: DRESS THE SHIP

All work and no play makes Jack a dull boy.

– English proverb

Jack needs to play even when he grows up to be a seaman. In his book *It's Your Ship*, Captain Michael D Abrashoff describes how he used to lighten the atmosphere on his ship. He would play music over the PA system once a week, and the crew would assemble to enjoy the music and watch the sunset together.

Leaders must help establish a pleasant atmosphere on their ships. For example, dressing the ship with multi-coloured flags streaming down the masts is an old nautical tradition. But it's about more than going through the motions. Celebrations and social events energise and strengthen teams. Whether it's a simple barbecue, swimming pool party, ping-pong competition, movie night, karaoke evening or dance competition, events can help uplift your team's morale. Remember: Your ship isn't just your workplace; it's your home away from home.

When I visit a ship, I often ask the crew when was the last party they had on board. The answer usually indicates the 'Happiness Quotient' of the ship. In all my years, I've found that happier ships tend to be better run, better maintained, and have fewer safety issues.

Crew on happier ships also get to know each other personally. This develops empathy within the team. When you know that a member of your team has some medical problems or is dealing with some personal issues, you understand the reasons for his behaviour better, and more importantly, you are able to help him when required. Closeness within the team means you all help charge each other up with positive energy.

On the old bulker, we took our visiting superintendent's advice and arranged a cabin contest. The cleanest and best decorated cabin was to win a surprise reward. There was excitement all around as the crew hustled to paint portholes and wash curtains. Later in the ship's lounge, one of the motormen was announced the winner. He took the box of chocolates he had won and shared it with everyone. It was heartening to see all our crew members in a positive, upbeat mood by the end of the evening.

We continued to familiarise and meet, train and drill together. As you may have guessed, we cleared the next port state control inspection without any deficiencies. Using all the right tools, our team had finally come together to form a cohesive unit, much like one strong rope.

But the story doesn't end here.

Following our inspection, we had another party to celebrate our success. It helped close our first chapter together – the one where we had lost focus and failed the inspection – and together begin a new one as a strong, tight-knit crew that was motivated to achieve even more in the future.

THE KNOTS AND SPLICES OF TEAM-BUILDING

- Teams don't form by themselves. They are spliced together using teamwork tools.

- Teamwork tools include:

  1   Familiarisation

  2   Meetings

  3   Drills

  4   Celebrations.

- The process of team-building is as important as the outcome of teamwork.

16

LEAD YOUR TEAM: AT THE HELM

*You have to create an environment where everyone is a leader.
That is, an environment where everyone works together, takes
the initiative, assumes ownership, is willing to deal with difficult
issues, and accepts accountability for the team's results.*

– Paul Gustavson and Stewart Liff, *A
Team of Leaders*

THE *HERALD OF FREE ENTERPRISE* was a ferry that regularly carried passengers and cars across the English Channel. Mark Stanley, the assistant bosun, was assigned the task of closing the bow doors of the ferry. Instead, he fell asleep in his cabin. Both his superiors, Terence Ayling and Leslie Sabel,[11] failed to check whether the doors had indeed been closed. Captain David Lewry saw Sabel on the bridge later, but didn't confirm if the doors were secured shut. And since he did not hear any unusual reports, the ship was all set to sail. Or so he thought.

When the ferry departed the Belgian port of Zeebrugge, waves began to lash the bow. This time, the ferry offered no resistance. With the bow doors opened, water began entering the car decks. Within minutes, the seawater sloshing around destabilised the ferry, violently flipping it over. The ship sank, eventually resting on the seabed. One hundred and eighty-eight innocent people died in this tragedy on 6 March 1987.

Investigations revealed that the shore managers were aware of previous occasions when these ferries had sailed with their bow doors open. The management of the ferry company had disregarded suggestions from captains to install warning lights on the navigation bridge. The company had also ignored reports of overloading of passengers. To say the least, the *Herald of Free Enterprise* was a failure in teamwork and leadership, from the assistant bosun to the captain and right up to the board of directors.

---

11 Terence Ayling, bosun; Leslie Sabel, chief officer.

When leaders don't create an environment conducive to teamwork, failure is inevitable. Communication and expectations will be unclear, and the crew will no longer hold themselves accountable to a high standard of work.

LEADERS CAN, HOWEVER, STEER THEIR TEAMS TO SUCCESS WITH THESE THREE KEY SKILLS:

1   Effective delegation
2   Supervision
3   Coaching.

1 EFFECTIVE DELEGATION: IT'S YOURS, MATE!

Lead by letting others lead.

– Senior Chief Matthew Skaggs,
Saltwater Leadership

Once, when I was on midnight watch, I noticed another ship approaching from behind on a collision course. Navigation rules at sea require the overtaking ship to keep clear of the one being overtaken. Now, the other ship was not following this rule, so I radioed its watch-keeper to alert him.

His response: 'I know the rule, but the captain ordered me to stay on the track line.'

I argued, 'Why don't you call him?'

'He does not like being called after midnight.'

Now, I was annoyed. 'Would you rather collide than deviate from the course? Would you like to be reported for violation of navigation rules?' Thankfully, he relented and hurriedly altered course, just in time to prevent a nasty collision.

The problem in this case was not just this navigator but also his captain. As a leader, he had failed to encourage his officers to take charge and respond to situations. Unless people are empowered, they will do only 'what they are told to do'.

There's no point trying to do everything yourself because you simply can't. You cannot work 24/7 nor do the job of 24 people. So, if you don't delegate effectively, you will eventually burn out.

You may feel that by delegating you're losing control. You may fear your team will make mistakes. And you might even enjoy the work you need to delegate, and therefore would rather do it yourself than spend time explaining how it's done. But how will holding on make you an effective leader? If you don't delegate, how will you find time for the things you need to focus on? And how will your team ever learn anything new if you're afraid to give them some level of independence?

> DELEGATION IS EMPOWERING YOUR TEAM TO TAKE THE DECISIONS THAT YOU KNOW THEY CAN.

If you want people to be responsible, let them feel responsible for the outcome. Realise that even your subordinates need some degree of freedom in decision making. More responsibility will boost their self-confidence, motivation and sense of fulfilment. Therefore, lead by letting others lead.

On the other hand, uncontrolled delegation like in the case of the *Herald of Free Enterprise* can lead to disaster. Simply making others feel accountable does not relieve you of the responsibility for the end result. For example, the second engineer might allocate tasks during an overhaul to different personnel, but he ultimately has to ensure that it's done properly. Delegating with a good sense of balance allows your team to work effectively.

Here are some strategies for effective delegation:

- Ask yourself: 'Do I have the time to do this job?', 'Is there someone available to whom I can delegate this?', 'How critical is the job that I have to do it myself?', 'How much supervision should I be doing?'
- Assign individual and group tasks clearly.
- Assess the people you choose. Check if the crew members are familiar and trained for the task. Check if you've assigned the right number of people for the job.
- Clarify responsibilities as well as the level of decision making. 'What should be reported, and how often?', 'What should be done if there is something out of the ordinary?'
- Recap. Ask your subordinate to repeat what he has understood about the task. A clarification can save a lot of time and headache afterwards.
- Discuss the time frame for reporting and completing the job.

- Encourage and guide. Let your team know that you are available for support and back-up.
- Determine beforehand at what stages you need to check in.
- If the completed work is not to your expectation, evaluate if the assigned person needs additional coaching.
- Follow up and follow through. Delegation is incomplete unless you have followed up on the completion of the task. Ask for positive confirmation. Double-check if required. No news is not necessarily good news – it could be bad news that hasn't yet been conveyed.

2 SUPERVISION: THE TELESCOPE

Be at the critical time and place; every day has (at least) one.

– Major John Chapman, US Army,
Muddy Boots Leadership

Once you delegate a task, the next step is supervision. Knowing when and where to be present is a skill every leader needs to develop. Chief Officer Sabel of the *Herald of Free Enterprise* should have supervised a critical operation such as the closure of the bow door.

Captain Joseph Hazelwood of the *Exxon Valdez* also failed in this regard. He left a tricky manoeuvre to Third Officer Gregory Cousins. Captain Hazelwood himself had earlier evaluated Cousins as possessing 'only average knowledge of ship handling characteristics'. If his intention was to help the third officer gain confidence in manoeuvring, he should have briefed him properly, highlighted the dangers, and stayed on the bridge to observe the execution.

Inadequate supervision can be just as disastrous in the engine room. The diesel generator of a reefer ship was damaged when its senior engineer failed to ensure that the bottom end bearings had been tightened to the right amount of torque. This generator powered the reefer containers on board. The damage meant the cargo of frozen meat worth hundreds of thousands of dollars was spoilt. Trust your colleagues, but do your own due diligence.

SUPERVISION HAPPENS ONLY WHEN YOU ARE PHYSICALLY AND MENTALLY PRESENT.

On another ship, contractors used the wrong spares during a turbocharger overhaul. Failure of the ship's engineers to supervise this task resulted in the turbocharger breaking down at sea. Better supervise than be sorry!

You should also realise that even the most willing seafarer may not have yet developed the expertise to carry out the job properly, or respond to any situation on time. Supervision is helping your team understand the nature of the job, sharing your experience, and clarifying what high standards you expect. Be patient and keep a watchful eye. Consistent supervision will give your subordinates confidence to do the job well, knowing that you're available to back them up.

Good supervision also means anticipating when you will need to be physically present. Captains will often mark on the chart when they would like to be called onto the bridge. Most chief engineers leave clear standing instructions, including an invitation to wake them up at any time: 'If you are in doubt whether to call me or not, then the time has certainly come to call me.'

Have an eye out for your team. Don't be so occupied with your own task that you can't supervise effectively. Officers at mooring stations have their own work cut out for them. At the same time, they must also make sure their crew is safe. This means ensuring that their crew are not exposed to whiplash from ropes, or the danger of crush injuries by moving hawsers.

Management By walking Around (MBA) is not only a great way to supervise but also a highly effective leadership tool. A leader needs to be visible, displaying his best behaviour, and communicating with his team. Many leaders don't recognise this, but team-members want to see and speak to their superiors on a regular basis. You cannot hide away in your office. Regular deck walks or engine room rounds convey that you are aware of what is going on and you are available for any feedback and guidance.

> SUPERVISION IS HAVING A SECOND SET OF EYES TO PICK UP WHAT OTHERS MAY HAVE MISSED.

Here are a few MBA tools:

- When interacting with other crew members, make it a one-on-one conversation, and one that's not necessarily all about work.

- Make these rounds a part of your daily routine, and vary your timings once in a while.

- Carry out focused inspections as part of your rounds to get the maximum out of your time.

3 COACHING: THE STEERING LIGHT

Coaching does not provide solutions; it helps with clarity. The answer lies within the individual; what a coach does, through question, answer and discussion is to find the answer the individual knows is there. The coach facilitates clarity of thought!

– Andrew St George, *Royal Navy Way of Leadership*

As captain, I often took a casual walk on deck after supper with the chief engineer. It was a relaxing routine, and it was also a good time to catch up with each other in a more informal setting. On one such walk, the chief engineer thoughtfully remarked to me 'I am having a problem with our new second engineer. As you know, he was promoted recently. But he's slow in picking up his new responsibilities. He doesn't know what his priorities are. I think he lacks the right attitude for the rank. Now I have to do his job as well.'

I reflected on this for a while, and then asked him, 'How long can you do his job, and when will you find time for yours?'

'I don't know. I've tried to improve his performance but I don't see any result.'

'How exactly did you try to improve his performance?'

'Ah. I called him to my room and told him to improve his work in one month, or else there would be consequences'.

'And has this approach worked?' Though he did not respond, both of us knew the answer to this was a 'no'. I continued 'Why don't you try coaching him?'

'Coach him? First of all, I don't get paid to do that. Second, I don't have the time'.

I challenged him, 'Weren't you encouraged by your senior officers back when you were moving up the career ladder? I certainly was. I still have the notes of my captain's sketches of how to manoeuvre in heavy seas'.

'Hmm … I see your point'.

'We are in leadership positions. We are paid to lead. We are not leading machines. We are leading people. You are already a good leader. Imagine how much more your team can achieve when you have also enabled those below you to succeed. When you help one of them, he knows you care. When he feels he is cared for, he will in turn care for the ship.'

We sat down on the bitts on the forecastle. I continued: 'Most people want to do well in their jobs but may struggle with new positions or unfamiliar tasks. They may not always come to us for advice. However, we would be failing in our leadership if we didn't help them. When we coach, we help them focus, learn new problem-solving skills, develop their confidence, and adopt new habits. You don't have to *teach* your Second anything; you just have to help him learn.'

'Okay. I understand an effective leader also has to be a coach,' he said. 'But how do I go about actually coaching him?'

'First, you have to believe that you are a good coach.'

He laughed. 'That's easy.'

'Next, you have to genuinely believe and show that your colleague has the potential to become better.'

The chief engineer let it sink in. 'Yes, my Second does deserve a chance. He's not such a bad guy.'

'Remember, this is not psychotherapy; you don't have to fix his personality. A good coach stays focused on improving the performance of his mate's tasks.'

'So I show him how it's done, right?' I could see by now that the chief engineer was beginning to accept the idea of mentoring his colleague. Now I just had to coach him to coach others.

'Yes, that's a start. Even better is to ask him first how he would go about a task. Then you ask him if he has considered a different approach. Explain how he could do it more effectively. A discussion is better than a lecture. In fact, good coaching is 80 per cent listening and 20 per cent speaking. Ask questions which help him reflect. Provide your insights where necessary to move the conversation in the right direction.'

'So, how will I know if he has understood?'

'Ask him to summarise. By the way, I can see from the smile on your face that you're enjoying our conversation.'

Laughing, he said, '*This* feels like a coaching session. I feel positive about all this, but I still feel uneasy about trusting him with more responsibility. What if he makes mistakes?'

'Let him know that you will monitor at all critical points. Coaching is very much a closed-loop process involving follow-ups and giving feedback. For some jobs he might need more time than you do. He may also make mistakes in the beginning. Guide him with patience so that he develops his confidence and skills.'

'How do you find time for all this? We are so busy in our daily tasks that there is no time for things like coaching.'

'Discuss only one issue at a time, for no more than ten minutes. The time you invest will save you a lot more time and effort later. Imagine if, with coaching, your second engineer became better at work; you would then have more time to spend on your own work.'

'That makes sense. But what do I do if he's not in the mood to listen? You can't force coaching down anyone's throat … can you?'

'You're right. People are emotional by nature; ergo, before starting, you must create an emotionally receptive mind-set. To do this, always start on a positive –te and compliment him for the jobs he's already doing well. Then move to areas where he could improve. A rule of thumb is three positives for every 'area of improvement'. And don't start coaching when you want to vent your frustration about a mistake he has made.'

'I see that the next level of leadership is about people, how to help them unleash their full potential, how to care for them, and how to engage them.'

'That's exactly it. So, how do you intend to apply this with your Second?'

'Let me see: create an environment of trust, take time out for coaching, identify what behaviours he needs to change, start with positives, ask him questions so he can reflect and find his own solutions, listen well, provide inputs where necessary, explain, show him if required, observe, supervise, and follow-up with feedback as necessary.'

'Brilliant! Just keep encouraging him. Tell him what specific things he's doing well. Sometimes a kind word is all people need to charge their day.'

'This reminds me – how does coaching work with our formal appraisals?'

'Good question. When you sit for appraisals, it should be like another one-on-one coaching session. They're more formal, though, where you record positives and areas for improvement for your team. It's also a good place to record training needs, so the personnel department can follow up. If you coach regularly, what you discuss during appraisals shouldn't come as a surprise.'

'Thanks, Captain, I learnt something new today. I'll let you know how it goes. Let's go and send those reports to the office.'

After this heartening conversation, I kept following up with the chief engineer on his coaching. Not only was the second engineer now better at his job, but also the chief's reputation as a leader was growing. He was now delegating and supervising more effectively. The mood in the engine room became even more positive than before. We were now able to complete machinery maintenance faster and with better reliability. Accident rates were down. Overall, our team was rocking!

The moment of truth came two months later; it was appraisal time. The chief engineer's comment about the second engineer was, 'He's an excellent engineer. I would love to have him on my team any time.'

This was personally satisfying for me and for both my colleagues from engineering. Being at the helm of my team had just become easier.

HOW TO LEAD YOUR TEAM

- A leader develops more leaders.

- Three skills for leading your team:

  1 Effective delegation

  2 Super supervision

  3 Coaching and mentoring.

- Supervision and delegation with a fine sense of balance allows you to do more, and do it safely.

- Coaching brings out the best in your people, and from your team.

17

COMMUNICATE FOR SUCCESS: BELLS AND WHISTLES

Silence in teamwork is not golden– it is deadly!

– Mark Sanborn, *You don't Need a Title
to be a Leader*

THE FILIPINO OILER on the container ship *London Express* noticed something unusual when he walked past the scavenging air receiver of the main engine. There was a red cotton rag sticking out of the engine door. At the time, he had been looking for the ship operations officer (SOO) as the ship was getting ready to leave the port of Savannah (US), and the SOO was nowhere to be seen. For a brief moment, he wondered if the SOO was inside this compartment.

A few minutes later, the oiler met the Filipino third engineer and the German chief engineer, and informed them about this unusual rag. However, he couldn't effectively convey his 'gut feeling' to them. On their part, the senior engineers didn't listen to him carefully enough. And they didn't bother to ask him any more questions. The red rag was a 'red flag' but no one acted on this cue.

About three hours earlier, unknown to anyone, the SOO had gone inside the scavenging air receiver for a quick look at the piston. When he entered, most likely a strap on his overalls caught the access door, causing it to slam shut. This sudden movement made the securing cleats fall into place, trapping the SOO inside. The walls were solid steel and no amount of shouting would be heard outside, in an already noisy engine room. As a final, desperate call for help, the SSO stuck a piece of red cleaning cloth through the slight crack in the opening. Unfortunately, no one responded to his distress signal, even as the ship sailed out of Savannah, assuming that the SOO had secretly deserted the ship. The SOO was found two days later, having succumbed to hypothermia.

The German Federal Bureau of Maritime Casualty Investigation found that the communication on the ship was not healthy, even *before* the accident. Both work-related as well as casual interactions on this ship were poor, thus hindering the free flow of information and trust between crew members. Added to this, there were several barriers to communication such as a strong hierarchical structure and age differences between the officers. The cultural differences between the German senior officers and the rest of the Filipino seafarers didn't help. As it always happens, the effects of poor interaction and unhealthy culture are magnified under stress. The SOO had to pay for it with his life, all because of poor communication.

WHY IS COMMUNICATION IMPORTANT FOR A LEADER? THE MORSE CODE

The art of communication is the language of leadership.

– James Humes, *Success Talk*

Four years after, and just 100 miles away from where the *Deepwater Horizon* met its fateful end, the offshore supply vessel *Tristan Justice* collided with an offshore platform. Fortunately, this time no lives were lost, and the environmental impact was limited to the escape of 22,000 cubic feet of natural gas; however, damages totalled around half a million US dollars. The reason for this accident? No communication.

During his navigational watch, one of the officers aboard the *Tristan Justice* noticed that one of the engine controls was not responding. His quick fix? He asked a deckhand to tie a cord to the throttle in the machinery space so as to keep the engine going full speed ahead. When the captain took over the navigational watch at daybreak, the officer did not inform him about the 'modification' he had made in the engine room. Nor did he brief the captain about the oil and gas rigs on the ship's path.

Minutes later, the captain was alarmed to see a gas platform appear out of the fog. It was only a few hundred metres ahead of him; the only effective collision avoidance action now was to reverse engines. He tried, but his actions had no effect as the throttle on the wheelhouse had been bypassed without his knowledge. He also tried changing the course, but it was too late to avoid the impact. After the crash, the platforms in the area had to be shut down for 20 days for repairs.

Words unsaid remain unheard. The main problem in communication is that which *doesn't* happen, just like the failure to pass on information at the change of watch on the *Tristan Justice*. It is estimated that over 60 per cent of all leadership problems are due to poor communication.

Every opportunity to communicate is an opportunity to lead. It is an opportunity to influence the success and safety of your team. Regardless of your position on the team, you have a responsibility to lead and to communicate. Why not aim to be good at it?

Every conversation is a means to share our expertise, energise our team, give clear directions, receive and give feedback, learn something new, and coordinate with our colleagues.

In fact, being able to communicate well is essential for our well-being. If we are unable to convey our views effectively, we allow emotional stress to build up. These unexpressed emotions result in anger and frustration. If we are not assertive, we may end up with an undesirable result. Good communication helps us forge relationships, and is key to a successful career and a satisfying life.

So, why do people not communicate enough? People have different personalities; some are naturally extroverted, some are shy. Some people hesitate to give bad news, or to express their concerns to a superior officer. Others are uncomfortable around some people and try to avoid conflicts. Sometimes, it's just that we don't want to look stupid in front of others.

Communication is an intentional act of leadership. It means that in spite of all our perceived hurdles and challenges, we're still able to connect with our team. It's about building trust. If a leader doesn't make an effort to engage with his team, how will the crew feel motivated on the ship? How will they know what they need to know? How will they respond in the way you need them to?

WHAT IS COMMUNICATION? THE WHISTLE

The effectiveness of communication is defined not by the communication, but by the response.

– Milton H Erickson, psychologist

Seven short blasts followed by one long blast on the ship's whistle signals emergency on a ship. The sound of it can mobilise an entire crew into action.

When rowing, the coxswain sets the rhythm for the rowers. It helps the boat move ahead faster.

Communication is flow of information whether it is a whistle, or a coxswain's beat, or us speaking with others. And it is also the subtle art of listening, asking, and being accessible. It is about energising your team, through speech, emails, or even your body language. It is about connecting with others for an effective response.

A captain once called me over the weekend, to inform me that there was heavy fog in port. He didn't feel comfortable manoeuvring in such unsafe conditions. As safety manager, I had to make a decision. The captain suggested we delay departure. After exploring other options, we agreed it was best to stay in port until the fog cleared, an estimated wait of six hours.

Through good exchange of ideas, we found a solution that was timely, effective, and safe. Making a collective decision was also less stressful than making the decision alone. Communication helps tap into your team's resources.

As with everything else we've talked about in this book, leaders can improve their communication skills with practice.

HERE ARE FIVE IMPORTANT SKILLS FOR EFFECTIVE COMMUNICATION:

1   Listen
2   Be quick
3   Be precise
4   Be courageous
5   Be respectful.

1 LISTEN WELL: SONAR

The most basic of all human needs is the need to understand and be understood. The best way to understand people is to listen to them.

– Dr Ralph Nichols,
International Listening Association

Had the senior engineers listened to the oiler, the SOO of the *London Express* might still be alive. They had heard the oiler's words but they did not listen to what he was saying.

Over 60 per cent of all our communication is about listening, so why not be great at it?

Simply hearing is not listening. Listening is active. Listening is making the other person feel heard, understood, and respected. Effective leaders build trust with their team with great listening skills.

It starts with being approachable. It is not just about having an open door policy, or letting your colleagues know that 'You can call me if you need me'. To be a good listener, you have to be accessible, so that people will feel comfortable speaking to you. If you have a reputation of being a bad listener, your subordinates will stop bringing their troubles to you. They'll go elsewhere for solutions, or worse, they'll let the problem linger until it blows up.

How can you become a better listener?

(i) When someone comes to you, let them know that you are ready to listen. Put aside whatever you are doing, and make eye contact.

(ii) Be engaged. Show them that you are listening with the occasional nod, or with phrases such as 'Go ahead' and 'I understand'.

(iii) Avoid interrupting with a 'No' or a 'But', or by looking at your watch. A moody or dismissive 'Yeah, I know' also discourages people. Never ever 'shoot the messenger' when he brings bad news. A leader should never feel irritated by interruptions; it may seem trivial to you, but your colleague may feel it is important. Leaders are paid to solve problems and interruptions are part of the game.

(iv) Take notes when appropriate.

(v) Asking him to tell you whether or not you have under-stood correctly, summarise what you have understood – and if necessary, ask him to explain it to you in more depth.

(vi) Finally, when the issue is clear to both of you, tell him what you are going to do about it. And always finish by thanking him.

Closed loop communication is a form of active listening that works well on a ship. For instance, unless the helmsman responds to a 'Starboard five' command by repeating it, there's no way of knowing that he heard it. It's a great technique that ensures the message is understood. And it's not limited to commands: after a pump room inspection, ask for a report and look for specific answers. Asking when, where, why, and how helps ensure that the information is complete and useful to you.

Observe the other person's expressions and tone of voice. If you spot signs of hesitation, ask more questions to clarify. Just like in navigation or in engineering, you rely on several sources of data, so in careful listening, you pick up on all the signals for information.

2 COMMUNICATE QUICKLY: TRANSPONDER

Keep people informed. Everyone wants to know what's really going on.

– Brian Tracy, *Motivation*

In teamwork, there is no such thing as sufficient information, or fast enough communication; it can always be better. That's what I learnt, but you'd better hear the whole story first. Once, when I was chief officer on a bulk carrier, I was having trouble pumping out the ballast tanks. The water had to be emptied to make room for the iron ore cargo, but now the loading was faster than the rate at which I could pump out the water. If I didn't solve the issue quickly, the ship could be over-draught or overstressed. But I was confident I could solve this complication and I was running between the engine room and the deck, trying to find a solution.

The captain, who was monitoring the draught of the ship, called me up on the radio. He wanted to know why we weren't keeping up with the cargo plan.

He was furious when I told him about the problem: 'I don't like surprises. I would like to be informed in time.'

I was confused. I was already handling the situation. I thought, 'What could he have done differently if I had informed him earlier?'

I got part of my answer when he suggested that we line up the tank valves differently because it helped speed up the deballasting rate.

The second part of the answer came later during the voyage, when we revisited the incident. This time he was calm.

'I can help in ways you may not know. For instance, I could have slowed the cargo conveyor until you had better control of the ballast. But you may not have necessarily thought of this solution as you were stressed and dealing with the problem at hand. My helping you *doesn't mean* that you have failed or lost control. It is my job to support you. But I can't help you if I don't know you need help.'

When you see a problem developing, communicate, no matter how small

DELAYED COMMUNICATION IS USELESS INFORMATION.

or insignificant it may appear to be at the moment. We often delay relaying bad news to collect more information, or wait to see if the situation improves. But this only gives your team less time to react. Over-communicating is any day better than under-communicating.

A ship's transponder is super-fast in sending distress signals, because when disaster strikes, every second counts. Speed is crucial, even in daily communication. When an officer calls the captain in a potential collision situation, every second decides if the evasive manoeuvre will be successful. When a crew member informs the watch-keeper about a leak in the cargo pipeline, every minute saves tonnes of oil from flowing overboard.

Timely communication is more credible than information offered after it is asked for; another lesson from the school of hard knocks. Once, our superintendent asked during his inspection why we had two generators running in port. Usually, one generator would have been adequate for our power requirements, and running two generators would increase fuel consumption. When the chief engineer explained that the generators could not be maxed due to technical problems, the superintendent became visibly upset. When he asked us why he had not been informed of this earlier, we struggled to explain ourselves. He then wondered out aloud what else we were not telling him. That day, both I, the captain, and the chief engineer lost some of our hard-earned credit, and it took us much more time to gain this credibility back.

3 BE PRECISE: THE BELL

It's a lack of clarity that creates chaos and frustration.

– Steve Maraboli, *Life, the Truth,
and Being Free*

When a bell rings on a ship, you know there's an emergency. You know you need to get ready for action. There is no ambiguity. Likewise, when communicating with others, ask yourself, '*Will my message be understood by him? Will I get the response I want?*'

Precise communication saves time. I learnt this when we ordered a motor for one of the deck winches, without providing all the necessary details. A series of emails followed: first, it was the purchase manager wanting to know the rating of the equipment, then it was the supplier asking for several other dimensions. When the motor finally arrived several months late, it was not ideal for exposed deck use. Apparently, somewhere among the innumerable emails that were exchanged, vital information was omitted. The entire episode had consumed so much of our energy that we wished we had done it correctly from the start.

Being precise is being complete. If the ship's speed is less than that required by the charterers, specify why in the noon report. Was it due to strong winds, or was it because of an engine limitation? Not doing so, you can expect a set of probing questions in your email the next morning.

Tell the truth. It can be unpleasant, but it's better than dealing with a nasty surprise later. Give all the facts immediately, even if it's bad news. And don't play it down or string it out piece by piece. Hiding facts and falsifying records corrode credibility. Speak the truth, even if your voice shakes!

Be direct. Be specific. Don't confuse the message with hints. When giving feedback to someone, don't just say, 'Good job.' Better to say, 'I was happy with the way you prepared the loading plan,' or, 'If the drums aren't secured, they could come loose in heavy weather. I want you to check them every morning and report to me.'

Precise communication is professional and it also applies to emails. Make sure your emails have appropriate subject lines, attach well-labelled pictures and diagrams, and always review before pressing 'Send'.

4 BE COURAGEOUS: THE GONG

Courage is what it takes to stand up and speak.

– Winston Churchill. British prime minister and first lord of the Admiralty. He is said to have recommended that oil be sprayed on coal to boost maximum speed on the steam-powered battleships

Korean Air Flight 801 crashed into a hill in Guam in 1997, killing 223 people. The investigation found that among many other things, the co-pilot was afraid to question the judgment of the pilot. Korean Air had a history of several such incidents, and they all pointed to one thing – a lack of courage to communicate.

This problem is also widespread in the maritime industry. A study found that even the most experienced ship's officers hesitate to intervene when they see a pilot making a mistake in the manoeuvring of a ship. It is no wonder that around 30 per cent of all collisions and 52 per cent of all groundings happen with both the captain and the pilot on the bridge. Such accidents cost the shipping industry at least 44 million US dollars per year!

This hesitation comes from the *assumption* that the other person – who is either more experienced or older, or both – knows what he is doing. Or that he does not need our input. We fear offending him with our opinion. We equally fear being offended in case he rejects our suggestion.

Courage is what makes our message as clear as the sound of a gong. If you think you are right, you must be assertive enough to express your view. A difference in opinions doesn't have to end in conflict. Skilful negotiation can convince others why yours is a win-win solution.

When in doubt, ask yourself, 'What is the worst that can happen?' We all possess the courage to speak up, but we suppress it when we are under stress, or when we want to avoid conflict. Be that as it may, you still have to summon the courage and speak instead of remaining silent. After all, you're doing this for your team and the ship.

'Encourage' your team to communicate. When Korean Air realised that people were intentionally avoiding their airline, they initiated a programme in the late 1990s to improve the communication skills of their aviators. Today, Korean Air is one of the safest, most profitable airlines. As crewing and training manager, I applied this strategy in our fleet and found success. I made it compulsory for assisting navigators to 'call out' to the captain during manoeuvres, when the officers have no option but to speak. The reasons for hesitation becomes less relevant. Now the navigator loudly alerts the captain before every scheduled change of course or speed, thus confirming that the ship is moving along the planned track. As navigators become more engaged with the manoeuvre, the captain is better aware of the various ship parameters. The captain now receives information of deviations well in advance so that he can take early corrective action if necessary. A simple but effective 'encouragement' has resulted in a dramatic improvement of our navigation safety.

5 BE RESPECTFUL: THE FLAG

You don't get anything by screaming and shouting at people.

– Commander Alec Perry RN, HMS *Illustrious*,
Royal Navy Way of Leadership

One of my least enjoyable periods at sea involved sailing with a captain who regularly yelled and screamed at us. The captain who succeeded him was a relief; he was respectful while also insisting on quality work. As an officer working under the two captains, I observed both styles of leadership, and the result surprised me. People followed the first leader out of fear, and the second out of respect. Guess who was more effective? And guess who inspired his team to work extra hours even when not asked to, simply because they didn't want to let their leader down?

Hoisting the host country's flag when in port is a mark of respect from the visiting ship. It enables the ship to carry out its business without interruption. Respect is the flag that allows a leader to succeed in his work while working with his team.

One of the basic demonstrations of respect is good manners. Good manners generate positive feelings and make others more receptive to what you have to say, even in a tough environment such as on a ship. 'Good morning', 'Thank you' and 'Please' are simple but effective communication tools. Research shows that people are positively influenced by a genuine smile or a polite word for several months after the event has occurred. And let's face it; you're more likely to positively respond to a respectful teammate than a grouch. So, remember to mind your manners, even in times of crisis.

Communication is not about pushing or ordering people to do more. Don't lose your composure, even when you have good reason to be upset. Sarcasm, insults, or abusive language is a strict no-no at any workplace. Instead, adjust your tone, moderate your language, and clearly explain why you are disappointed. And be aware of your body language. Your stance and physical gestures should never be intimidating or threatening, even in a heated conversation.

A golden rule for respect: Praise your colleagues in public, and correct them, when required, in private.

Sustained anger is never a resourceful state for a leader. An angry email or a cynical remark made in haste can damage your professional image and cause you to lose respect in the eyes of your peers. Instead of responding quickly, I've found that pausing and counting backwards from 20 helps me calm down whenever I'm angry. I never send an email when I'm upset. I may write a rebuttal, but I save the draft until the next morning. Then, after my initial anger has ebbed, I assess the most constructive way to communicate. It helps me when I avoid taking criticism personally and try to look at the situation from the other person's perspective.

Respectful communication is also about rapport. For instance, when our pilot came on board, we would offer him a cup of hot tea and discuss the manoeuvre. In return, he would invite us to let him know if the ship deviated from the planned track. On the one occasion that I intervened, he was glad that I was watching his back. At the end of the day, we could continue on our voyage safely. This is what teamwork is all about.

LET'S COMMUNICATE

- In Golden Stripes teamwork, silence is not golden; it is deadly.

- Communication is not about ordering and pushing. It is a subtle art of listening, making conversations, and bringing in your team together towards common objectives.

- The responsibility to effectively communicate always falls on the leader.

- Key communication skills

    1   Listen; 60 per cent of our communication is listening

    2   Be quick; speed is crucial

    3   Be precise; report the complete facts

    4   Be courageous; clearly voice your opinions.

    5   Show respect; build rapport.

THE FLANGE MODEL©: THE NUTS AND BOLTS OF TEAMWORK

Just as nuts and bolts connect flanges together, teamwork tools help a crew work together, safely and efficiently. Use this aid-to-memory when working with your team.

The Flange Model

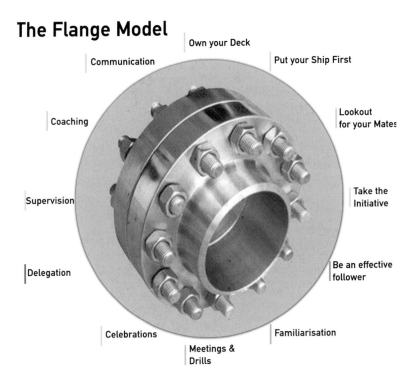

Own your Deck

Communication

Put your Ship First

Coaching

Lookout for your Mates

Supervision

Take the Initiative

Delegation

Be an effective follower

Celebrations

Familiarisation

Meetings & Drills

18

SAFETY MANAGEMENT: THE LIFEJACKET

Safety is not an intellectual exercise to keep us in work. It is a matter of life and death. It is the sum of our contributions to safety management that determines whether the people we work with live or die.

– Sir Brian Appleton (on the explosion of the oil platform *Piper Alpha* in 1988 that killed 167 people, including 2 rescue crew)

MY COLLEAGUE 'CHANDRA' was boiled alive.

The chief officer had asked him and the bosun to paint the exhaust pipes on the funnel. The ship was going to stay at anchor for a day. The timing was perfect for working on the vent stacks because the engines were cool.

At the time, Chandra was just an ordinary seaman. Unknown to him and the bosun, a boiler survey was in progress in the engine room. As a part of the survey, the boiler would be pressurised until the safety valves were activated at a pressure of 11 bar. When the boiler finally reached its limits, it let out the excess steam at full force. The steam was over 300 degrees Celsius. Its only exit was a vent on the funnel. Chandra was working directly in front of this vent, and he never saw it coming. He bore the brunt of the scalding steam.

His skin turned translucent white. He was in shock. We would lose him if we didn't act fast. Fortunately, the ship was within helicopter range of one of the world's best hospitals with a burn care centre.

BE SAFE. DON'T END UP AS A STATISTIC!

Chandra suffered over 90 per cent third-degree burns. He had to battle for his life and the long and painful recovery took several months. His skin was scarred but his spirit was not.

This kind of trauma usually makes people hang up their sea boots for good. But Chandra was better than average – he turned out to be an extraordinary seaman. Undaunted, he was back sailing a year later. He recently obtained his navigator's licence and currently sails as a second officer on an ocean-going ship. He's also happily married and is well respected within the company.

Not all such stories have a happy ending.

I have had my share of injuries, too, and have had to respond to many more. I'm always saddened to hear of any injury on a ship. However, the particularly gruesome nature of Chandra's accident completely shook me.

Most accidents in workplaces indicate a gap in the leadership of safety management all along the organisational chain. My team and I prayed for Chandra. At the same time, we brainstormed for ways to avoid any recurrence of such accidents. How could we improve our systems? How could we effectively implement these systems?

The more incidents we analysed, the more we understood. Eventually, we would establish a powerful set of safety management tools and initiate several training programmes. We developed a robust safety culture that would uphold and sustain standards in the shipping industry.

You and I are not alone in this challenge. The global commercial shipping industry faces a growing list of safety concerns.

- Around 1,000 seafarers suffer fatal injuries every year.[12] The death rate among seafarers is higher than in nearly every other comparable industry. For example, 12 times higher than in heavy manufacturing.[13]

- On average 127 large ships were lost every year, between 2005 and 2015.[14]

- *Sewol, Costa Concordia, Rena, Smart,* and *El Faro* were some of the recent high profile accidents. Claims resulting from the *Costa Concordia* tragedy were over 2 billion US dollars, and that from the *Rena* were over 450 million US dollars.

- 214 large oil spills were recorded in the two decades from the late 1990s, resulting in a loss of around 234,000 tonnes of oil.[15]

---

12 International Maritime Organization (IMO).
13 Baltic and International Maritime Council (BIMCO).
14 Allianz Safety and Shipping Review 2015.
15 The International Tanker Owners Pollution Federation Limited (ITOPF).

- Since the year 2000, around 70 seafarers have faced criminal sentences for wilful breach of environmental regulations.

The message is clear; shipping is a high-risk industry. Accidents are the number one reason for commercial delays, losses, and damage to reputation. Navigation accidents cause more loss of life than any other type of incident, such as a fire on board.

Enforcing an effective safety management system as well as dynamic safety leadership is as vital for our lives *as much* as it is for staying in business. Therefore, managing risks and avoiding accidents is the *number one* priority in shipping.

WHAT CAUSES ACCIDENTS? FIRE IN THE HOLD!

Most accidents originate in actions committed by reasonable, rational individuals who were acting to achieve an assigned task in what they perceived to be a responsible and professional manner.

– Peter Harle, director Accident Prevention, Transportation Safety Board of Canada, and former RCAF pilot

Why do accidents still occur? After all, no one willingly gets injured, collides their ship with another, or pollutes the sea. But while will is one thing, knowing what to do to prevent an accident is another.

There are two direct causes for accidents: hazards and risks.

A hazard is a source of danger, such as hot vapours from a ship's funnel. It may exist all the time, or it may be present only occasionally. If I don't shut down the boiler before working on the funnel, I allow the possibility of steam to be released at any time. I allow the hazard, or unsafe condition, to exist.

Risk is when I willingly or unknowingly expose myself to a hazard. When I send my team to work on the funnel without completing the safety checklist, or without protective gear, I am acting unsafely. I am putting my team at risk of getting scalded by steam.

Allowing hazards to exist, or taking unnecessary risks, is an accident waiting to happen.

HAZARDS AND RISKS? THE DEVIL AND THE DEEP BLUE SEA

In almost every kind of hazardous work, it is possible to identify typical accident patterns.

– Dr James T Reason, human error expert

Fog at sea is a hazard. Sailing through fog bears the risk of collision with other ships. Radar reduces this risk by detecting targets even when they're not yet visible to the naked eye. Training the navigators in anti-collision manoeuvres reduces this risk further.

Conversely, fatigue in a navigator increases the risk of him making a mistake in avoiding an oncoming ship. The faster the speed of the ship in fog, the higher the probability of a collision, and the greater the consequences. Therefore, risk increases or decreases depending on our actions.

Will our actions be consistent every day? Will the different crew members that control the ship every few months act in the same safe way? You know as well as I do that maintaining such a high level of consistency is very challenging.

This is where safety management comes into the picture. It is a combination of organisational philosophy, policies, procedures, training, recruitment, and decision-making, all of which aim to make people behave in the same, consistent, safe manner.

SAFETY IS DOING A JOB RIGHT, THE FIRST TIME AND EVERY TIME.

Safety management is the effective detection of hazards and the management of risks. If you cannot avoid a hazard, reduce the risk to an acceptable level so that you can work safely – whether it is sailing through fog, or working on a funnel.

Safety is the desired result of controlled actions against identified risks. Safety is keeping out of the devil's way without falling into the deep blue sea.

PREVENTING ACCIDENTS SYSTEMATICALLY: THE LIFEBUOY

A bad system will beat a good person every time.

– W Edwards Deming, quality management expert

It is said that unsafe acts cause most accidents. Specifically, it is said that over 80 per cent of accidents are caused due to human error.[16]

I view things differently. I prefer a variant of Deming's theory: Over 80 per cent of accidents are *systems related*.[17] I prefer this line of

---

16 Reason, J., (1997), Managing the Risks of Organizational Accidents. Aldershot: Ashgate.
17 W. Edwards Deming, American engineer, has said that 95% of variation in the performance of a system (organization) is caused by the system itself and only 5% is caused by the people. Figures modified by author based on his own observations and analysis.

thinking because a system can be fixed (rather than trying to fix all the people around us!). Issues around training, familiarisation, unsafe acts, unsafe conditions, competency, and to some extent even motivation and communication, are system-driven and are therefore fixable.

'People issues' such as inattentiveness or misjudgment cause the remaining 20 per cent of accidents. Because there are many more people than there are systems, addressing individual performance is always going to be a challenge. That said, we have already addressed the techniques to learn and master what you don't already know in Chapters 6 and 7, so I won't repeat them here.

Maintaining and improving systems is a proactive, long-term process that can greatly reduce risk. It's also a more positive approach than waiting for things to go wrong and subsequently blaming people for their mistakes. But we can improve systems only when we understand the systems in question well. After all, it is we people who can make a system fail or succeed.

Some people see safety management as burdensome paperwork, but this is more out of ignorance than based on facts. Safety management is much more than just procedures and checklists.

Over the years, the International Safety Management (ISM) Code and tighter regulations have made ships safer for their crews and friendlier for the planet. When you hear talk about 'the good old days' when there were almost no systems, it's easy to see how the ISM Code has brought in a positive change:

- The number of ships lost at sea (total losses) has *decreased* by over 40 per cent in the last 20 years.[18]

- The number of seafarer deaths has *decreased* by over 50 per cent since the ISM Code was introduced.[19]

- The number of oil spills (of over 700 tonnes) has *reduced* by around 92 per cent over the last 40 years.[20]

One accident is one too many. Ergo, every step we take to understand, implement, and improve safety management systems is a step towards safer ships and cleaner oceans.

In my experience, systems are best explained using analogies and visual models. One such illustration is Abraham Maslow's Hierarchy of Needs. His pyramid framework makes a considerably complex theory of human motivation easily understandable for most of us. Similarly,

18 IUMI, International Chamber of Shipping.
19 IHS Fairplay, International Chamber of Shipping.
20 ITOPF, International Chamber of Shipping, this refers to oil spills of over 700 tonnes.

I distilled the otherwise complex systems of safety management by creating a simple analogy, based on the video game Pac-Man.

A NEW MODEL OF SAFETY: THE 'SAFE-MAN' GAME!

Think of risks as surprises.

– Preston G Smith and Guy M Merritt,
Proactive Risk Management

Who doesn't love video games? One of the most popular games in the 1980s featured Pac-Man eating dots around a maze, and four devils (Blinky, Pinky, Inky, and Clyde) trying to catch and destroy Pac-Man. In those days, I particularly enjoyed playing this game on rainy days at the only game arcade in my native Port Blair. Below is my model of safety based on Pac-Man.[21]

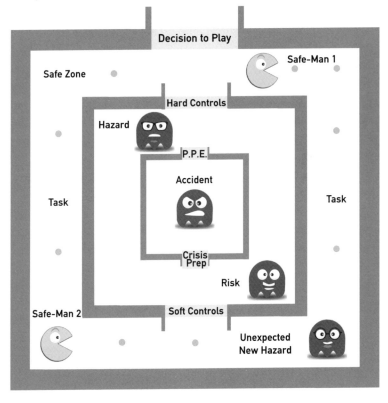

The Safe-Man Game Model of Safety ©

21 You can play the game for free at http://www.freepacman.org/. The game is also now part of the motion picture *Pixels*, Sony Pictures, Columbia Pictures, 2015.

Imagine yourself and your fellow crew members as Safe-Man 1 and Safe-Man 2. Before you begin any task, you have the option of considering if it is really necessary to begin right away. For instance, you may ask, 'Can we delay going on deck until the weather has quietened?' Once you have decided that there is no other alternative but to begin the task, the game starts.

The game is to fulfil a task, such as navigating in restricted visibility, overhauling a liner, or carrying out a ballast tank inspection. If you heed all the available safety precautions, you can work in the 'Safe Zone', where the risks are reasonably low.[22]

SAFETY IS THE DESIRED RESULT OF CONTROLLED ACTIONS AGAINST IDENTIFIED RISKS.

Now, three of the devils (Hazard, Risk, and Accident) are locked behind barriers, while one (Unexpected New Hazard) roams free trying to catch you by surprise. If a barrier fails, *presto* – the nearest devil inside it is released. This means that now you have a second devil to contend with. When you have more than one free devil, the 'Safe Zone' is no longer safe, and it's only a matter of time before they move in for the kill.

Throughout the game you have to watch out for the other members of your team. Because if any of the devils catch even one of your crew (Safe-Men), the game ends.

To ensure that you have a safe day on board, give each Safe-Man a play zone with low risk, control the devils as best as you can, be alert for the free devil, and show your crew how to play to win.

WHERE ARE THE DEVILS? ICEBERG AHEAD!

The greatest trick the devil ever pulled was convincing the world that he doesn't exist.

– *Usual Suspects*, the movie

In my early days of seafaring, I did not know about the many dangers at sea. Despite my long career, I am still introduced to new ones every day. These dangers were always present; it's just that I was unaware of their existence until I met them face to face.

I know now that we can only identify these hazards through

---

22 The common industry phrase for this 'safe zone' is ALARP (As Low As Reasonably Practicable).

expertise and focused examination, and from discussions with our colleagues. Safety bulletins help. Accomplished leaders are usually avid readers, which helps them and their teams stay aware of most devils.

When a hard control[23] barrier is compromised, the hazard devil from my Safe-Man safety model is free to move into the Safe Zone. When the soft controls are ineffective, the risk devil is released. These two controls are the most potent barriers, and if we neglect them, even the best protective equipment or emergency response cannot ensure safety at sea. Without these two barriers, the probability of an accident becomes very high.

If an accident should occur, it is the final (innermost) barriers that determine how serious the accident will be. If a seaman is not wearing protective equipment (PPE), an injury is a likely outcome. If the crew is not prepared to effectively respond to an emergency (Crisis Prep.), the consequences of a fire can be very serious.

The best way to play the game is to keep all safety barriers intact and the devils within them. If we don't implement the controls, it is one mariner versus many hazards and risks. Even for the best player, it becomes a tough game to play.

The Unexpected New Hazard is always present in the game; even in the Safe Zone you do not know when this devil will come into play. The only way to avoid this danger is by staying alert and responsive.

The *Titanic* didn't see the iceberg until it was too late. But the ship could have slowed down to reassess the situation. They should have been asking, 'Is everything OK? Should we be concerned by the iceberg reports?' On a ship there is no special alarm to warn us of a developing danger. On the *Titanic*, chronic unease, or a constantly questioning mindset, could have helped the navigators stay alert, identify the Unexpected New Hazard, and respond to it well in time.

SWITCH OFF THE BREAKER, AND SWITCH ON THE 'SAFE-MAN' MINDSET

A prudent man foresees the difficulties ahead and prepares for them; the simpleton goes blindly on and suffers the consequences.

– *The Bible*, Proverbs 22:3

I met Jeno at a firefighting course in 1995. He was a young electrical trainee then, full of energy and enthusiasm. We kept in touch for a short while after the training, but gradually we heard less of each other

---

23 For more on hard and soft controls, see 'Safety controls: the Safety Shoe' below.

as we got busy with our own lives. A couple of years ago, I came to know through a common Facebook friend that he had died.

He was an electrical officer on a ship when it happened. He had climbed on top of the ship elevator to fix a problem. Unfortunately, he didn't switch off the breaker to the elevator. Switching off the breaker would have ensured that only he could operate the elevator, from inside. Nor did he post warning notices that work was in progress. He met his end when a steward, unaware that Jeno was standing on top of the elevator, pressed a button to summon the elevator.

Jeno was taken by surprise when the lift moved up unexpectedly. He had no time to react. A second later, his head struck a steel stiffener in the elevator shaft, killing him instantly.

Risk comes from not knowing what you're doing. Safety is when you are aware of and can effectively manage risks. Switch on the 'Safe-Man' mind-set. Before any work, ask:

'What are the risks?'

'What can go wrong?'

'How can we control the risk?'

Your level of expertise will determine how effectively you answer these questions. And as the saying goes, 'two heads are better than one'; whenever possible, ask your team to provide inputs, so you can leverage their collective knowledge.

Keep the lines of communication open; other team members may know of hazards that you don't. A team meeting and a simple risk assessment are still the best ways to safely begin any task. They also ensure that others don't put you in danger. Had the steward known about the maintenance work, Jeno would still be alive.

But what happens if you don't have time for completing a formal risk review? What do you on the spur of the moment?

HOLD IT! TAKE TWO!

Take calculated risks. That is quite different from being rash.

– George S Patton, 'The Old Man',
US Army general

I once acted rashly and nearly lost my life.

I was assigned to forward stations to release the anchors as our tanker manoeuvred into the anchorage. I ordered the anchor crew to release the brakes, but this had no effect. I then instructed them to fully open the brakes and shake the handle. Still nothing.

The back-up option was to lower the anchor using power. But this time, the ship was short on fresh water, and to conserve every drop we had left we had shut the steam supply to the windlass. The captain sounded impatient on the radio, as the ship was drifting away from the planned anchoring position. I was now under huge pressure and running out of time.

Stressed and without a second thought, I grabbed a heavy steel rod, stood on top of the windlass, and began hammering away at the anchor chain. Moments passed and the anchor was still stubbornly stuck to the ship. Suddenly, there was a rumble, and the anchor chain started moving. Before I could get off the windlass, the chain picked up speed.

By this time, the entire winch was shaking as the cable furiously paid out into the water. I stood awkwardly, with my legs on either side of the chain reel,[24] careful not to lose my balance. A cloud of rust and mud rose around me.

After what seemed like ages, the chain was fully released, falling silent. I climbed down, acutely embarrassed, and much to the amazement of the crew around me. They all knew, as did I, that I was extremely lucky I hadn't been dragged down with the chain to the seabed.

I beat the risk devil that day, but just narrowly. You don't always have time to complete a risk assessment form in such situations, but you can always do a Take Two.

Take Two is when you pause for a second thought, when you stop for two minutes and think about what could happen. It's a quicker version of a risk assessment when you think by yourself or, better still, discuss with your shipmates how the risks can be reduced.

When faced with such situations, you must resist the urge to get the job done or just rush to help. Over 50 per cent of enclosed space deaths have occurred when a seafarer hurried to save his colleague without concern for his own safety. In most such tragedies, the seafarer was overcome by toxic gas even before he could reach his colleague. On a commercial plane, you'll be familiar with the emergency procedure that instructs passengers to first put on an oxygen mask over their own face and ensure their safety before trying to help anyone else, even if it's their own child sitting next to them. Such is the case when you're at sea. If you forget your own safety, a 'quick' job or rescue could

---

24 Also called the 'gypsy'.

become your last job. This is why every mariner must put his own safety first, and supervisors must stop their subordinates from doing anything rash. It only takes two minutes.

SAFETY CONTROLS: THE SAFETY SHOE

The time for taking all measures for a ship's safety is while still able to do so. Nothing is more dangerous than for a seaman to be grudging in taking precautions lest they turn out to have been unnecessary.

– Admiral Chester A Nimitz, US Navy

There's a secret to winning at the safety game: You must put on your *safety mindset* before you put on your safety shoe. If you keep danger within the safety controls and complete all tasks successfully, you live to play another game. Let's introduce you to the controls.

(I) DECISION TO PLAY OR ABORT: SHOULD WE OR SHOULDN'T WE?

Deciding what not to do is as important as deciding what to do.

– Steve Jobs

Decide whether or not to perform a task immediately. Because yes, you have a choice. Therefore, question everything:

'Should I even expose my team to the hazard?'

'Can we avoid the area of heavy fishing traffic by steaming five more miles away from the coast?'

'Can that overhaul be carried out when the crew is not fatigued?'

'Is it possible to repair that pipeline by taking it to the workshop instead of welding it onsite?'

'Should I slow down to avoid the area of very high waves?'

'Can I delay the departure from port until the visibility clears up?'

If you can't remove the hazard, and you must complete the task right away, the next step is to assess how you can minimise the associated risks. Only play the game if you are confident of winning.

(II) HARD CONTROLS: SETTING THE ALARM

If the sensible suggestion that indicator lights be installed had received, in 1985, serious consideration which it deserved ... the disaster might well have been prevented.

– Formal investigation into the sinking of the *Herald of Free Enterprise*

Once you decide to take a calculated risk, or play the game, you need some safety controls to pull the ship out of port. After all, ships are meant to sail, not sit in the harbour.

First, prepare the work environment by setting up the hard controls or engineering controls. Hard controls keep the hazard devil within bounds. Lock out the boiler and the engine before working on the funnel. Ensure the gas detector is calibrated before entering the tank. Switch on the 'dead man' alarm, to sound if the navigator dozes off during his watch. By using hard controls, you eliminate unsafe conditions, set up warning systems, and make the work environment safer.

SOLAS[25] and Class Rules[26] have progressively helped eliminate risks at sea. Pollution risks were minimised by segregated ballast tanks being required on tankers. Single point failures were reduced by making duplication of critical systems compulsory, such as for steering and main-engine lubricating systems.

When we fail to maintain these systems, we create unsafe conditions. I know of a case where the chief engineer removed the circuit board on the oil-mist detector alarm to prevent it from going off at night. During the early hours of the following morning, the oil vapour made contact with a hot spot in the crankcase and caused a huge explosion. A crew member was killed, and the ship was adrift at sea and out of operation for weeks.

At least three hard controls had failed on the oil platform *Deepwater Horizon*. The failure cost 11 lives, 17 serious injuries, damage to the environment, and ultimately, BP having to pay over 53 billion US dollars in damages.

(III) SOFT CONTROLS: CHECKLIST

Risk management is about people and processes and not just about models, forms and software.

– Trevor Levine, risk management consultant

---

25 Safety of Life at Sea Convention, by the International Maritime Organization.
26 Classification societies, or recognized organizations, which ensure ships are built and maintained to certain standards, usually on behalf of a flag state.

Soft controls are people- and behaviour-focused measures that can help you avoid unsafe acts. These administrative controls include procedures and checklists that help the Safe-Man avoid the risk devil.

Training, fatigue control, communication, and supervision are also soft controls that help the Safe-Man stay alert and to avoid the unexpected new hazard devil.

During one of my auditing assignments on a ship, I was reviewing the departure checklist. The steering check required that the officer record the time the rudder took to move from one side to another before *every* departure. I was taken aback to see that the second officer had written '28 seconds' as the answer, and then simply photocopied the form. The checklist had been completed *without* actual verification. A safety control had been ignored. I explained to him the reason why the timing needed to be recorded each time: 'A delayed rudder response is an indication that there is something wrong with the steering system.'

Simple procedural omissions such as improper testing of steering and propulsion engines, poor filter maintenance, inadequate draining of water from fuel tanks, and incorrectly set engine trips are the usual causes for ships to lose control in congested waters. The cost of such lapses are almost always in millions of dollars.

The young officer admitted that he hadn't even realised that something was wrong until I had pointed it out. Hopefully, the ship was now a bit safer than it was before I boarded it.

(IV) PERSONAL PROTECTIVE EQUIPMENT (PPE)

Safety Gear – 2 minutes, Risk Assessment – 5 minutes, a Mishap with loss of life or limb – forever.

– Common safety slogan

PPE are the last barriers against personal injury. They help reduce the effects of any new hazards. Helmets, overalls, gloves, safety glasses, safety shoes, life vests, fall arrestors, safety belts, life jackets, chemical suits, gas masks, hearing protectors, welding aprons, insulating gloves, and face shields are all types of personal protective equipment.

If a seaman is not wearing his PPE, the accident devil can strike at any time.

Use them appropriately. The third officer on the chemical tanker *ECE Nur K* lost his eyesight and suffered chemical burns when a clamp on the cargo hose parted, forcefully splashing caustic soda on his face.

The investigation revealed that he was not wearing the required safety equipment for handling this strong chemical cargo.

Safety at sea is the business of all hands. Don't wait to be reminded to wear your protective gear.

(V) CRISIS PREPAREDNESS

Good risk management fosters vigilance in times of calm and instils discipline in times of crisis.

– Dr Michael Ong,
Illinois Institute of Technology

At sea, dangers lurk everywhere, even when you think you are working in a Safe Zone. If you are attacked by an Unexpected New Hazard, only your crisis preparedness will determine if the outcome will be a near miss or an accident.

Being prepared for an emergency is one of the basic aspects of seamanship. It comes from thinking ahead about what could go wrong and what you could do to prevent matters from escalating.

The crew of the *Costa Concordia* and the *Sewol* were not prepared for emergencies. They could not evacuate the passengers in time before the ship capsized. Had they been prepared, several fatalities could have been prevented.

A DANGER FORESEEN IS HALF AVOIDED.

The emergency response on the *Deepwater Horizon* oil platform was delayed by around 40 minutes, and wasn't as it should have been. The Safe-Men, sadly, were overcome by the accident devil. Game Over? Unfortunately, yes.

Do everything to keep your ship and your team safe. It is not enough to go through the motions. There is no such thing as being 99 per cent safe. It is either 100 per cent or nothing. It would have made a difference to Chandra!

PROACTIVE SAFETY MANAGEMENT

- All accidents can and must be prevented.

- Hazards and risks cause accidents.

- Safety management is the elimination of hazards and the management of risks.

- Risk assessment hinges on the essential question 'What can go wrong?'

- Take-Two to ensure that you do not act rashly.

- Safety management systems keep dangers under control. Remember the 'Safe-Man' game!

- Removing the source of danger. Hard controls, soft controls, crisis preparation, personal protective equipment (PPE) and constant alertness keep the Safe-Man safe.

19

SAFETY LEADERSHIP: THE FUEL

Culture has pervasive effects that can not only open gaps and weaknesses, but also, and most importantly, it can allow them to remain uncorrected.

– Dr James Reason, human factors expert

IN 1998, THE CAR-CARRIER *EURASIAN DREAM* was unloading its cargo at the port of Sharjah, UAE. While one of the cars was being jump-started, the spark ignited the gasoline being poured into the carburettor. This caused a minor fire, and it should have been extinguished immediately. But that is not what happened.

It took the crew almost an hour to activate the fixed carbon dioxide (CO_2) extinguishing systems. Even then, the gas-tight doors were left open and the CO_2 simply dissipated into the atmosphere without controlling the fire. The ship became a floating inferno and had to be towed to sea to let the fire burn itself out. By the time the drama ended, the ship and its cargo worth millions was just a floating pile of scrap metal.

Irked by this fiasco, the cargo owners sued the ship owner for damages. The lawyers argued that the management and the crew had been incompetent. To start with, allowing the dangerous practice of jump-starting a car while refuelling was a serious failure in supervision.

The crew's response to the crisis was woefully inadequate. The fire extinguishers that could have put out the fire when it was still small were poorly maintained. Resources such as radios for internal communication were insufficient. The crew was not familiar with the ship and was not fully prepared to handle emergencies. In fact, the judge hearing the case referred to the actions of the chief engineer (he closed the wrong fire extinguishing system valve) as 'idiotic'.

How did the *Eurasian Dream* actually become a nightmare? It was not one, but a progression of many small lapses which combined to create one flaming failure. Training and drills had not been carried out effectively. On the first Sunday of the month at a pre-determined time, the crew of the *Eurasian Dream* would muster for a drill. They lacked the ability to act spontaneously, and this showed when they had to fight an actual fire. In the end, the judge ruled against the ship owners. He agreed that the safety culture on the ship was poor and that the leadership of safety had failed.

Safety leadership is the fuel that gives the energy for a strong safety culture. This culture sets the rules for the game, guides the actions of the players, and it drives its results. A vibrant safety culture means robust safety barriers, better trained Safe-Men, and greater chances of playing more rounds of the game. Safety culture is not a destination, but rather a journey, and the course is shaped by its leaders – that includes you.

THE SAFETY CULTURE: THE ENERGY FOR THE GAME

A culture of safety starts with leadership, because leadership drives culture and culture drives behaviour. Leaders influence culture by setting expectations, building structure, teaching others and demonstrating stewardship.

– Rex W Tillerson, Chairman and CEO,
Exxon Mobil and 69th US Secretary of State

An expert trainer and ship inspector once told me, 'I know from the moment I am at the reception of an office or at the gangway of a ship how my day is going to be. Even among ships of the same company, I can sense the difference.' I understood. He was talking about the culture of the ship. Not so easy to define, but not at all difficult to see and feel.

What is a culture? You could say 'It's the way we do things around here!' And you would be mostly right. A safety culture is not what is written in the manual; it is what we do with what's written in it.

Any culture is established by beliefs, behaviours, and reactions to events. The culture can be seen and felt by the way everyday activities are conducted, by how people interact with each other, by how leaders lead and communicate, and by the (often unwritten) code of ethics applied in an organisation.

Think for a moment about the culture in your work environment.

Why is safety culture so important? Research explains that workplaces with a healthy culture are 49 per cent less likely to have accidents and 60 per cent less likely to make errors in their work. The culture of our workplace is the energy that influences the quality of what we do and how we do it, even when no one is looking. It influences how well written procedures are actually implemented. In other words, without a good safety culture, not even the best manual can make a work environment safe.

Remember the Pac-Man analogy in the previous chapter? Well, the game also has power pellets, or energisers, which once eaten by Pac-Man weaken the devils while gaining him more points. Similarly, a robust safety culture is the energiser which helps the Safe-Men carry out their tasks every day, while keeping dangers at bay.

> A SAFE CULTURE INFLUENCES SAFE BEHAVIOUR, EVEN WHEN NO ONE IS LOOKING.

Like all good things in life, a good safety culture doesn't just happen. It requires intentional leadership to create, maintain, and inspire such a culture. In fact, every member of the team should feel enthusiastic, even overzealous, about their safety culture. This is where safety moves from the realm of safety management to safety leadership.

For a culture of safety to flourish, it must be supported at all levels throughout the organisation, but it begins with Golden Stripe leadership. Here are my seven leadership strategies for a strong safety culture:

1   Create symbols
2   Open feedback channels
3   Use hands-on risk management
4   Share stories
5   Enforce routines
6   Reinforce
7   Decide 'safety first'.

Pick up all seven energy packs for a strong safety culture.

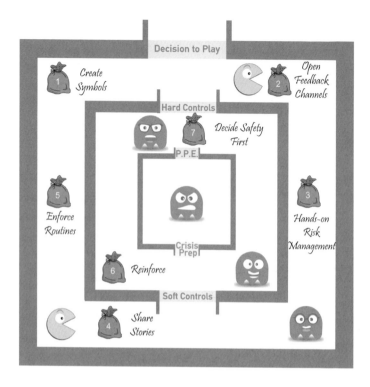

Safety Culture - The Energy for the Game ©

SEVEN STRATEGIES FOR A STRONG SAFETY CULTURE

1 CREATE SYMBOLS: THE FUNNEL

We are symbols, and inhabit symbols.

– Ralph Waldo Emerson, poet

Just like the tail logo of an aircraft tells us a lot about it, when we look at the funnel of a ship we immediately know which company the ship belongs to. Because the funnel is usually the best-kept exterior part of the ship, it also symbolises the condition of the rest of the ship.

Symbols send a strong visual message about the culture of a workplace. A safety culture's strongest symbols are its leaders. How a Golden Stripes mariner carries himself, how he dresses, what safety gear he wears, how he acts, and how well he communicates, all reflect the culture on the ship.

Become a symbol of safety and create more symbols. Insist on a clean and tidy ship. Good housekeeping inspires safe mindsets. Insist that your team wear safety gear, because it clearly demonstrates the behaviour you expect. Don't forget to put up safety posters and safety signs – they show enthusiasm for what you believe to be important.

2 OPEN FEEDBACK CHANNELS: FROM TUNNEL TO FUNNEL

The day the soldiers stop bringing you their problems is the day you stopped leading them. They have either lost confidence that you can help them or concluded that you do not care. Either case is a failure of leadership.

– General Colin Powell, US Army

It's quite obvious that safety issues should be discussed during safety meetings. But how it actually happens depends on a lot of things. Take the case of one such meeting where the fitter reported that the engine room crane was not safe for use. This made the chief engineer defensive. He was furious that a piece of equipment under his charge was being reported as defective. I immediately tried to calm him down:

FREE AND OPEN COMMUNICATION IS THE FOUNDATION OF A SAFE WORK ENVIRONMENT.

'He's just reporting a defect. Let's investigate and fix it. That's better than having an accident to deal with. Don't take it personally.'

Thankfully he took my advice and we were able to constructively address the concerns of the fitter. The crane got its due attention and remained trouble free for many months thereafter.

I've seen that unsafe conditions aren't always reported or noticed by senior officers. Junior officers and ratings might notice them first as they are the ones working at the frontline. This is why you should ignore hierarchy when receiving feedback. Simply receive the feedback and give it the importance it deserves. And be prepared for bad news, because it's the leader's job to deal with it. When you're warned early about a problem you're able to fix it in time.

For the message to reach from the tunnel to the funnel, you must also create an open reporting culture which encourages team members to share information about safety problems without the fear of being blamed for it. This means publicly thanking the seaman who brings up the issue, addressing and acting on suggestions within a reasonable timeframe, addressing personal issues in private, and highlighting good behaviour. This sends the message that everyone's feedback is valued and respected. In turn, your crew will feel more valued, committed, and responsible for the ship's safety as well as their own.

3 'HANDS-ON' RISK MANAGEMENT: MAINSAIL

The visible commitment and enthusiasm of the leader is the single most important influence of safety culture.

– Successful Health and Safety Management, HSE UK

One of many captains that I've sailed with, Captain William Zheng, once provided me an invaluable insight in managing risk. We were in Durban, South Africa, and had planned to lower the lifeboat into the water. It was my first experience with this boat model, and I was confused about how to operate the hook mechanism.

Sensing my discomfiture, and without being asked for help, Captain Zheng came down to the lifeboat, explained the procedures, showed us the movements, asked us to repeat it in his presence, and then let us lower the boat into the water. He also spent some time talking about the dangers and how over a dozen deaths had occurred in the last decade due to the wrong operation of levers. The few minutes he spent with us had a lasting impact on my view of how leaders influence the culture of a team.

Senior officers typically have more experience than their shipmates, which means they have relevant inputs to share when planning a task. It then becomes the duty of a Golden Stripes mariner to lead others with his knowledge – and to do it effectively, what better way than being 'hands-on'?

4 SHARE KNOWLEDGE: SEA STORIES

Experience is the best teacher. A compelling story is a close second.

– Paul Smith, *Lead with a Story*

Every time I tell people about Chandra's ordeal on the funnel, the audience is emotionally moved. Stories make it easier for us to remember lessons from our earlier mistakes. They help us identify which behaviours can cause us harm and which can keep us safe. Stories inform us of the dangers to look out for.

I also love to share positive stories, whether I'm speaking to the crew on a ship or at a company seminar. Just as Aesop's fables have long inspired children and adults, stories on how accidents were prevented or the day was saved enlighten us on which behaviours influence positive outcomes.

When you share real-life incidents, people can relate to the circumstances and the characters. They better understand the choices available, and the decisions that are acceptable within that safety culture. Stories also create a shared sense of identity and belonging. So, when you tell a story about what a good result looks like, it can inspire the team to change the culture for the better.

The added benefit of storytelling is that it creates a knowledge-sharing culture. It's is one of the most effective ways to transfer information within a group. Stories capture the essence of a company's policies and make them memorable. Stories help colleagues warn each other about the devils they have seen; they convey lessons and insights that go much deeper than a speech on the theory of safety; and they fuel discussions and debates that spark new ways of thinking and revitalise the safety culture

5 ENFORCE ROUTINES: POLISHED BRASS

They had learned that true safety was to be found in long previous training, and not in eloquent exhortations uttered when they were going into action.

– Thucydides, *The History of the Peloponnesian War*, 404 BC

Routines are set patterns that sustain a culture. They confirm to members of a team that their system is not only in print, but also in action. Routines do to a culture what polish does to brass. If you stop polishing brass, it becomes dull over time; similarly, if you do not enforce routines, your safety culture will fade away.

Familiarisation, training, drills, safety meetings, accommodation inspections, and safety equipment tests strengthen the soft controls and test the hard controls. These routines help the Safe-Men avoid the devils.

But routines don't happen by themselves. A leader has to commit his own and his team's time for these routines. He has to prioritise safety routines in his team's working schedule. So you need to schedule challenging, yet realistic, training activities on a regular basis. It may be tempting to put off that meeting or drill because you are busy, but beware of letting the routine slip.

On the *Eurasian Dream*, the crew would muster at a pre-determined time for an 'emergency drill'. They would go through the motions just for the sake of paperwork. The drill had become like a mere stroll in the park. Then, one day, during an actual fire, no one knew what to do; it was 'run for your lives'. And the ship was lost.

6 REINFORCE: GANGPLANK

The culture of any organization is shaped… by the worst behaviour the leader is willing to tolerate.

– Steve Gruenert and Todd Whitaker,
educational leadership experts

A few months ago, I attended an industry seminar and heard a young officer talk about his first year at sea. One of the incidents that he narrated caught my attention:

'One of our ABs was known to routinely disregard safety procedures. One day the captain, who was on his daily rounds, saw the AB working without a helmet. We were certain that the captain would discipline the seaman, but to our surprise the captain simply walked on.

'The captain's silence gave us the impression that the AB's behaviour was acceptable. Within a matter of days, the rest of the crew also began to get careless about safety procedures and protective gear. They left their helmets in the locker room when going on deck. Shortcuts became commonplace. People became sloppy.

'A few days later, one of deckhands fell overboard and died. Given the poor safety culture on board, I wasn't surprised to learn that the deceased seaman hadn't been wearing a safety belt. In spite of written procedures on what gear was required, the culture no longer supported safety. By ignoring the cowboy conduct of the AB, it had become the captain's mistake, and a disastrous one at that.'

Until about two centuries ago, sailors who breached discipline on board were publicly flogged, keelhauled or even made to walk the gangplank. The punishment sent a strong message to the rest of the crew. Thankfully, these barbaric methods are no longer employed in modern-day seafaring. Leaders, however, still have the responsibility to send a clear message when they observe a violation on the ship. You only achieve what you reinforce.

Hold everyone – yourself, your subordinates, and even your superiors – to a high standard of behaviour. Don't accept anything less. Correct *immediately*; don't leave it for the next time. A leader must be aware that despite best intentions, a procedure may be disregarded, either out of ignorance or wilfully.

Sometimes, people may violate a rule because they're not aware of it. This can happen when the crew is given new types of jobs for which they're not trained or briefed. Chandra, for example, wasn't aware that he had to take certain additional precautions on the funnel; the chief officer, however, was expected to know, and do his due diligence. As a leader, you can never assume that your team knows as much as you do; you must look out for, and stop, improper behaviour.

TRUST IS IMPORTANT IN A TEAM, BUT WATCH OUT FOR VIOLATIONS. REACT STRONGLY TO DISCOURAGE RECURRENCE.

Other times, people take shortcuts when they're fatigued or stressed. A shortcut saves time and effort, which is an instant reward, and that is the usual incentive for such risk-taking. You start by thinking 'Let's do it, just this once. Why bother making a big fuss?' So you bend the rule a bit, and before you know it, you allow a culture where rules are regularly broken. And lives are lost. Be aware of these impulses, in both yourself and your crew. Make it clear that rules are not a matter of convenience.

We can also become careless when we're bored. Boredom sets in when we lose interest in familiar and monotonous routines. Complacency and disinterest show through statements such as, 'I forgot to do it', or 'I didn't see it'. Leaders need to clearly voice their displeasure at acts of carelessness. Send a clear message that such lapses are unacceptable in a professional environment. Insist that things are done right the first time and every time.

The worst kind of violations are those done wilfully. Engineers have been known to pump out oily waste at sea because they thought no one was looking. More often than not, these engineers simply didn't want to change their (old) way of doing things. Unfortunately for them, they not only ended up in prison for these violations, but their companies were also held liable for the actions of their engineers, and had to pay out million-dollar environmental fines. The AB who didn't wear his helmet probably thought, 'What's the big deal?' Observing his poor example, the rest of the crew also discarded their helmets, simply because 'everyone was doing it'.

YOU ACHIEVE WHAT YOU REINFORCE.

In such cases, you must react strongly. Sometimes it means disciplinary action, other times dismissals, but it has to be done in the interest of preserving the safety culture for the rest of the crew.

As a leader, you must deal with safety deficiencies in a clear, decisive manner. Investigate all safety violations, near-misses, and accidents. The worst thing to do is cover it up. Making someone 'feel the gangplank' for lack of due diligence is acceptable. At the same time, those making genuine errors can be let off with a warning. And use good judgment in deciding between a wilful action and an honest mistake.

7 SAFETY FIRST DECISIONS: TO SAIL OR NOT TO SAIL

A commitment to safety should not be a priority, but a value that shapes decision making all the time, at every level.

– International Association of Oil and Gas Producers

Most ships are required to be dry-docked (out of water) twice every five years so that their keel, rudder and propeller can be inspected. This time is also used for major maintenance work, and the repairs are planned several months in advance. Every effort is made to ensure that the ships safely finish the repairs, on time, within budget, and so that the ship will not need any more major maintenance for the next two and a half years.

During one such docking in China, three days before we were due to sail, the fourth engineer came into our repairs meeting with a worried look. When the steel around the tank was being sand-blasted (to remove rust), a weak spot had been found on the fuel tank boundary. We were faced with a dilemma: we could go ahead with the repairs, and it would cost us three extra days; or we could leave it unattended, and risk the weak spot springing a leak during the voyage.

> OUR DECISIONS TODAY ARE THE STRONGEST INFLUENCE OF OUR TEAM'S BEHAVIOUR TOMORROW.

The rest of the crew and the shipyard workers watched on as the chief engineer, the superintendent, and I sat down to discuss. We eventually decided: the steel plate had to be changed.

When they first heard it, our colleagues in the commercial department were upset. A delay would mean that the booked cargo would be carried on another ship. The additional repair work would cause us to exceed our docking budget. Yes, there was a price to pay for the delay, but we were assured of the safety of the cargo during the voyage. Later, we got word that our colleagues in commercial were pleased that we had taken a difficult yet brave decision. When the story got around to the cargo shippers, the insurers, and the rest of the fleet, everyone knew we had placed safety first, over all other considerations.

More so than words, your decisions will define how much you value safety. These values are what will guide future decisions and determine the strength of the safety culture.

The Transocean rig crew and the BP's well-site leaders on the *Deepwater Horizon* detected signs of a breach of the integrity of the oil well. Still, the pressure test was accepted. The leaders in charge didn't consult with each other. Hours later, a deadly explosion set off one of the largest and most expensive oil spills in history.

A leader has to balance both commercial and safety priorities. A decision made in the interest of safety can sometimes be unpopular, but a leader has to have the conviction to stand by his decision.

As a leader your commitment to the safety culture is tested when it's time to make difficult decisions. Be aware that every single decision you make will influence the behaviour of the rest of your team. Use your professional judgment, and where time permits consult with your colleagues, to keep safety first!

So there you have it – safety is a game that must be played to win. Losing is not an option. You now know the rules and the objective of the game – Chandra needs to be safe!

LEADING THE SAFETY CULTURE

- Safety Culture provides the energy for the safety game: managing risk and staying safe, every day. Developing and sustaining it is a leadership responsibility.

- Seven effective steps for a strong safety culture are:

    1   Symbols

    2   Feedback channels

    3   'Hands-on' leadership

    4   Stories

    5   Routines

    6   Reinforce

    7   Decide 'safety first'.

- Unsafe acts and violations must never be accepted. They must be discouraged in clear terms.

- The leader has to carefully balance both commercial and safety priorities. Safety is always the 'first' priority!

20

DECISIVE LEADERSHIP: TRUE NORTH

Nothing is more difficult, and therefore more precious, than to be able to decide.

– Napoleon Bonaparte,
emperor of France, 1804

IN NOVEMBER 1997, the refrigerated general cargo ship the *Green Lily* was loading frozen fish at the harbour of Lerwick in the Shetland Islands. The night before their scheduled departure, the captain looked up the weather forecast. It did not look good. The report predicted stormy winds of up to 55 knots. The ship was designed for engine speeds under 19 knots.

The captain had a tough decision to make. If they delayed departure, the ship would reach Abidjan, Ivory Coast, a few days later than scheduled. If they sailed now, they would have to contend with monstrous waves whipped up by the storm.

Though the data in his hand did not indicate otherwise, the captain estimated that the wind speed at sea would not be more than 30 knots. Since he had sailed through similar conditions before, he felt it was safe. As a result of this faulty assumption, he decided to leave port. As soon as the ship left the shelter of the harbour, the captain realised that his decision to sail was a poor one. The ship was tossed around by the furious waves, and the propeller raced when it came out of water. The chief officer fractured his leg while trying to secure some of the ropes that were awash on the quarterdeck. The captain still had a choice of returning to the safety of harbour, but unfortunately did not do so.

Things got worse when the engine was unable to take the force of the battering waves. The engine tripped into over-speed, and the ship was now at the mercy of the waves. A few hours later, the ship crashed on to the shores of the Shetland Islands. A rescuer lost his life while trying to save the lives of the crew.

SECTION V: THE COMMAND THAT MATTERS

Decisions. Our expertise, our motivation, our alertness, our teamwork skills, and our safety leadership – all culminate in the decisions that we make. In spite of all good plans and intentions, we may still face ambiguous and unfamiliar situations at work. Each situation is unique. How should we respond in each such case? There are no standard answers. Nevertheless, as a Golden Stripes leader, you are responsible for the high-stakes decisions.

A shocking result from research asserts that most people fail at decisions at least half the time. This we cannot afford at sea. Effective leaders always know which decisions are important, and have acquired a good sense of judgment to make the right decisions. So can you.

First, we need to know why we err in our judgment. We don't make poor decisions on purpose. So, why do people make so many wrong decisions?

THE CARDINAL (SINS) BUOYS OF DECISION MAKING

All decisions are human – there's no machine to make them for us – and history tells us that the greatest decision always involved a combination of human genius, passion, determination, and foibles. Emotions flared, for good and ill.

– Dr Deepak Chopra,
endocrinologist and author

Cardinal buoys mark wrecks and dangers at sea. Likewise, there are markers which can help you avoid error-inducing mind-traps as you go about your voyage making those critical decisions. For decisions are not just based on data but are also influenced by our state of mind, and poor decisions in particular are influenced by our subconscious state of mind. Ergo, you have to use your *conscious will* to avoid these mind-traps. Be aware of these traps, and you'll keep your leadership from wrecking decisions.

1   Hubris
2   Assumptions
3   Indecision – freeze
4   Avoidance – flight
5   Imprudence.

1 HUBRIS: MUDDY WATERS

Facts do not cease to exist because they are ignored.

– Aldous Huxley, author

The *Royal Majesty* was a modern passenger ship, carrying an array of the latest navigation equipment. The navigators used GPS data as the primary means to check the position of the ship. During the voyage, the GPS antenna wiring came loose, and the electronic chart display began to display incorrect positions of the ship. A small alert flashed on the corner of the display, but it was ignored by the officers on watch. The ship was slowly but steadily moving away from its planned track.

Buoys and shore marks would have indicated that the ship was off course, but the navigators ignored these signs too, for 26 hours. The officers were *surprised* when the ship suddenly grounded at dinner time, 17 miles from where they were supposed to be. Obviously, if the officers weren't even aware that something was wrong, how could they have decided on the right corrective action?

Hubris means a loss of contact with reality and an overestimation of one's own capability. At work, it's easy to feel that everything is all right and lose awareness that change is occurring. Situations move from normal to critical without a clear boundary, and without warning. New risks and challenges develop all the time. It's your responsibility, and yours alone, to be aware of the situation at all times.

Stay alert and adaptable. A sense of chronic unease helps. No news is not always good news. Had the officers asked themselves if the GPS was OK, they would have cross-checked the ship's position using land features. If they had scanned the chart screen carefully, they would have seen the alert flashing in the corner. They would have realised the *Royal Majesty* was heading into danger. And they would have taken a decision to change course.

2 ASSUMPTIONS: THE FOG

Assumption is the mother of all screw-ups.

– Wethern's Law of Suspended Judgment

You and I have to process a lot of information every day; how should we respond to each piece of news, and correctly decide? How can we get through this fog of data without getting lost?

On an otherwise normal day a junior engineer I know informed his chief engineer that the sounding of one of the fuel tanks had dramatically reduced. How did the chief engineer respond to this news? He assumed this to be a sounding error, and did not take any action. Two days later, another crew member found fuel in a cargo hold. Fuel from this very fuel tank had escaped through a hole into the adjoining hold. Ten containers filled with pasta from Italy, worth a few hundred

WHEN YOU ASSUME, YOU MAKE AN ASS OUT OF YOU AND ME!

thousand dollars, were destroyed. I'm sure you will agree that no pasta could ever taste good in *that* type of sauce!

In ambiguous situations, our subconscious mind makes assumptions so as to quickly make sense of the situation. For instance, if we see a junior engineer with dirty overalls, we automatically assume that he has been working on machinery. If his eyes are red, we may assume that he has not slept enough. While such assumptions may provide context to our observations, they cannot substitute facts. This makes assumption a very weak basis for making important decisions.

It was easy for the chief engineer to assume that the junior engineer's report was wrong simply because he had no other explanation for it. His assumption fogged his professional judgment. The wise approach would have been to independently verify the facts, and then to decide what to do.

People tend to make assumptions when they have incomplete information. They use assumptions to fill these gaps in awareness, thus creating a poor interpretation of reality. Ship collisions have time and again occurred because the navigators thought they had the right of way, each navigator assuming that the other would steer clear of his ship.

Furthermore, we make assumptions more often than we think we do. Most of our assumptions are about people. Since we cannot always read their minds, we are quick to form our opinions about them. We rush to judge people, and that makes us either accept or reject their inputs too quickly, without sufficient reason, and solely based on our assumption of them. The chief engineer made the same mistake with his subordinate's input, and this clouded his decision-making ability. The consequence was 200 tonnes of toxic pasta.

ASK YOURSELF IF YOU ARE ASSUMING SOMETHING. VERIFY.

The trick is to be *conscious* of our natural tendency to make assumptions. Make a deliberate effort to verify the facts. Be curious. Ask questions. Clarify. If you have to decide immediately, and you do not have sufficient time to collect all the information, it is okay to make calculated assumptions, but allow for safety margins. Even with calculated guesses, err on the side of caution.

Assumptions are the fog over the horizon of situational awareness. If you want to make better decisions, your conscious mind needs to win over the subconscious.

3 INDECISION: FROZEN WATERS

Indecision is the graveyard of good intentions.

– HA Hopf, German mathematician

Freeze. That's what my captain did when our ship lost steering while under way in the river.[27] He didn't know what to do when faced with an unexpected challenge. He was afraid. He became anxious because his next action would determine the safety of the ship and the course of his career.

When we feel fear, our hardwired instincts kick in. We either freeze, or fight, or take flight. Which one do you tend to pick?

Picking the right instinctive response is what determines our ability to decide effectively.

Flight is running away from the situation, and freezing is doing nothing at all. At sea, both these responses mean indecision. Not deciding when we need to is also a wrong decision. Indecision however, does not make the problem go away; it only delays the inevitable or even makes it worse. Eventually, you will have to deal with the situation, but with less time and fewer options.

Indecision only makes easy things hard and hard things harder. Instead of being proactive, when we let things become urgent, we make poor decisions. How many times have we seen navigators postpone collision-avoidance manoeuvres, only to take more complicated evasive measures later? How many cases of delayed preventive maintenance have turned into hurried breakdown maintenance?

A common symptom of freezing is

TO DECIDE IS YOUR DUTY, AND ACTION IS BETTER THAN INACTION.

---

27 See introductory chapter.

believing that problems will resolve by themselves. But wishfully thinking that the weather will improve won't alter the course of reality.

Another common excuse you can hear from indecisive people is 'if it ain't broke, don't fix it' (often said convincingly).

This is the reason why preventive maintenance is often delayed – that is, until troubles start to show. Instead of proactive and systematic upkeep, people are forced to work overtime on repairing breakdowns. And, instead of taking responsibility, indecisive people then blame the problem on the situation.

Inaction also happens when we wait too long for more information. We wait it out so as to make a perfect decision. But instead, this becomes indecision if it means action is not taken in time. Captain Smith of the *Titanic* wanted to get to New York on time while also avoiding the ice. He had the best intentions, but inaction sinks all intentions. He waited too long to find out the exact location of the icebergs. Instead, he should have decided to reduce the vessel's speed as soon as he was informed of the danger in the vicinity. Understand that you will not always have all the information you need, but you will still need to decide then and there. Time and tide never waited for anyone's decision.

4 AVOIDANCE: ABANDON SHIP!

You can avoid reality, but you cannot avoid the consequences of avoiding reality.

– Ayn Rand, author

Flight. Extreme examples of this psychological response are the actions of the captains of the *Costa Concordia* and the *Sewol*, who chose to escape rather than find a way to save the passengers from their sinking ships. Similarly, we also tend to put off decisions and bury our heads in emails or routines. But avoiding the stress of making a decision won't make the issue go away.

Leaders need to bust stressful situations with strong decisions.

Fear, lack of confidence, and unwillingness to take responsibility for a decision can also lead to procrastination. We resist making decisions by thinking 'What if I carry out that overhaul and something goes wrong? Will I be blamed?' Procrastination may save us temporarily from making a decision, but it also leaves us without any real options later. It is easy to shrug off responsibility by saying 'there was only one option – we tried, and it didn't work'. But this is not how leaders think.

Strong leaders take strong action at the right time. Fear of criticism is a telling factor why some people avoid decisions. But if you have observed due diligence and arrived at a well-considered decision, there's no reason to fear criticism. Very often, it will be an unfamiliar situation, and you will need your professional instincts to guide you. Don't worry about erring in your judgment. We learn *more* from bad decisions than we do from plain indecision.

Decision making is a muscle that you have to build and maintain with practice. The more decisions you make, the better you will get at it. Start with intentionally making small, prompt decisions every day, and over time you will build your capacity for bigger decisions.

5 IMPRUDENCE: RHUMB LINE

When answers are not readily available, grabbing on to the first
thing that seems to offer relief is a natural impulse.

– Paul C Nutt, author, *Why Decisions Fail*

The chief officer on the chemical tanker *Bow Mariner* had a problem. He had to get 22 tanks cleaned and ready for cargo in two days. Safety procedures require that tanks be fully ventilated before the crew can clean them. Short on time, he ordered his crew into the tanks even though there still were hazardous gases (from the previous cargo) inside.

When a subordinate officer protested, the chief officer brushed him aside with a disdainful: 'I have to do it, I can do it, so I will.' A while later, a spark ignited the flammable vapour in the tank. An explosion followed, and the ship sank, killing 21 seamen.

The chief officer had made an imprudent decision. He wanted to get the tanks ready in time at all costs, even at the cost of safety. It never works this way; imprudence and seafaring don't go well together. Every decision calls for a balance of priorities. *How* we achieve our goals is as important as achieving them or not. Bad decisions always let us know that we were wrong, sooner (most likely) or later.

Risks don't change just because there's less time available to do the job. Don't rush just because you have a decision to make. Taking a shortcut 'just this once', or assuming that consulting with others will make you appear weak, are mind-traps that the prudent mariner needs to avoid.

Consult with your colleagues and superiors. Seek multiple views. As discussed in previous chapters, you don't, and shouldn't, make all the decisions by yourself. Had the chief officer of the *Bow Mariner* asked the captain for more time to gas-free the tanks, he might have been given it. Had the captain of the *Green Lily* consulted with his office, he might have delayed departure until the winds reduced. Take time to evaluate different options.

Rhumb line navigation is the easiest way to sail between two points while maintaining the same bearing relative to true north. But this is not always the shortest or the safest route. There are other factors to be considered, such as depth of water, safety margins, and weather. Similarly, when you are making a decision, you need to carefully assess all possible consequences for all the people affected by your decision.

KEY TO GOOD DECISION MAKING: THE RIGHT HEADING

Truly successful decision-making relies on a balance between deliberate and instinctive thinking.

– Malcolm Gladwell, *Blink*

All was well and in the blink of an eye, it wasn't. This is how the pilot on the car carrier *Hoegh Osaka* must have felt. The ship was departing the port of Southampton, UK, with its precious cargo of luxury cars, when it suddenly listed heavily to one side. The ship soon lost steering and propulsion, swung to one side of the channel, and ran aground.

There was no time to investigate the reason or to recalculate the ship's stability. The pilot made an instinctive decision to keep the ship aground until further assessment could be done. It was an effective decision under the circumstances, as it saved the ship, the lives of the crew, and most of the cargo.

If the pilot and the ship's officers had taken longer to decide or had acted rashly and pulled the car carrier out, it might have capsized. It could have blocked the entrance to the port, causing severe disruptions to the flow of trade.

Effective decisions make effective leaders. A good sense of judgment can be developed through intentional practice, a positive mindset, and the courage to make decisions.

When faced with an ambiguous situation, we can either see it as a threat or as an opportunity to execute responsibly. Subdue feelings of 'freeze and flight'; instead,

WHAT IS THE WORST THAT CAN HAPPEN IF I DECIDE? WHAT IS THE WORST THAT CAN HAPPEN IF I DON'T?

tap into your primal 'fight' response to decide and act. Thinking about it won't remove fear, but action will. Muster the courage, decide, and act.

Develop a mindset for making decisions.

Start with small goals at your workplace and achieve them. Even fulfilling personal goals such as completing a round of physical exercise can also help in building your decision-making muscle. Successful results will give you the confidence to make more decisions. When in doubt, ask yourself, 'What's the worst that can happen if I decide? What's the worst that can happen if I don't?'

Trust yourself.

'What if I am wrong?', 'Do I have proof?' Questions of doubt and 'what-ifs' confuse the mind. Courage is not the absence of fear, but it is the will to decide and act despite the uncertainty of the outcome. Trust your professional judgment, your intuition, and your opinion. If you don't trust yourself to make the right decision, no one else will.

Decide as many things as early as possible. This means planning in advance when you're not under time constraints. Anticipate the decisions you will have to eventually make:

'What will be my speed when I execute a turn in this harbour basin?'

'In which port can we carry out the overhauls? How much time will we then have for the job?'

When planning, also visualise emergencies or a back-up course of action. Ask yourself:

'What will I do if my engines fail during the manoeuvre?'

'What am I going to do if I find a damaged piston ring during the scavenge space inspection?'

Dealing with a difficult situation becomes easier once you have foreseen the possibility and trained for the response. Being prepared makes it easier to decide.

A NEW TEMPLATE FOR DECISION MAKING: DECIDE

Decision is the spark that ignites action. Until a decision is made, nothing happens.

– A Peterson, The Art of Living Day by Day

A power card indicates the status of combustion in a diesel engine. It is also an effective decision support tool, because it tells the engineer what adjustment or maintenance is required. Similarly, I found the DECIDE template, originally developed in the aviation industry, a useful decision support tool for any workplace, even at sea.

DECIDE – Detect, Evaluate, Choose, Identify, Do, and Evaluate effectiveness.

(D) DETECT

A leader has the ability to recognize a problem before it becomes an emergency.

– Arnold H Glasgow, businessman and author

The captain of the *Green Lily* failed to detect that the conditions were rapidly deteriorating.

You cannot really anticipate everything. You simply cannot know what kind of situation will arise or what you might face on a ship. Be prepared to be surprised or confused. Be prepared to respond swiftly – while manoeuvring, in seconds; at sea – within minutes.

Detect that there is a change in the situation. Detect the risk at hand. Ask yourself:

'What is the situation here?'

'What does my professional instinct tell me?'

'Have I seen or heard about something similar before?' Visualise how the situation could develop further.

Research shows that there is a strong correlation between stress levels and decision making. Effective management of stress brings the clarity to detect change and act. Alertness sharpens your instincts. Always trust your instincts.

Prepare for unfamiliar situations and be ready to innovate. Even the best plans have to change in the face of reality. The worst thing you can do at this point is to carry on as if nothing has happened. So be ready to adapt. Realise that it is time to decide.

(E) EVALUATE

Crew members will never be able to rely exclusively on procedures, however well designed, and must therefore be properly trained and adequately prepared to handle unexpected circumstances with the same level of safety as they handle routine operations.

– Loukia D Loukopoulos, R Key Dismukes, Immanuel Barshi, *The Multitasking Myth, Handling Complexity in Real-World Operations*

The captain of the *Green Lily* made evaluation errors. He assumed that the winds would be weaker than predicted. He put himself under pressure to sail out of port. To justify his decision, he allowed himself to believe that the situation was safe, though it was not.

The difficult decisions are usually those closer to the boundaries. A common trap people fall into is stretching these boundaries instead of conducting a rational evaluation. I can't say that stretching boundaries never works out, but ask yourself if it is worth the risk.

The captain's second error was not including the rest of his team in evaluating the situation. He could have asked for the opinion of his crew and the shore office so as to make a well-considered decision. The decisions made after an unsatisfactory negative pressure test on the *Deepwater Horizon* suffered from exactly the same errors in evaluation.

Evaluate systematically and analytically. Look for additional sources of information. Be aware of any emotions that may interfere with your evaluations. Consult with others when you have the time.

(C) CHOOSE

It is not always possible to have the ideal outcome, but it is pragmatic to have the best possible outcome under the circumstances.

– Anonymous

The captain of the *Green Lily* had two choices: delay sailing or depart on schedule and take his chances with the weather. It was a choice between commercial loss or safety. He chose to sail, the ship was overcome, and in the end everything was lost. The decision did not make sense either way.

Choose your actions wisely. There is no procedure for everything, but your priorities will guide you. Schedule or safety? The answer is always safety of life. Commercial losses or loss of time considerations are secondary. When in doubt, err on the side of safety.

Decisions seldom are about choosing good versus bad. So an ideal outcome in all decisions is rare. It is often a choice between good and better, or bad and worse.

The first course of action should be as prescribed in the Safety Management Manual; override this only if you have a good reason to do so. Do not violate procedures under pressure unless for safety reasons. And do not make a rash decision for decision's sake.

(I) IDENTIFY

An expert is someone who has succeeded in making decisions and judgements simpler through knowing what to pay attention to and what to ignore.

– Dr Edward de Bono, psychologist,
inventor of Lateral Thinking

A chief engineer once heard the oil mist detector (OMD) alarm while the ship was at sea. He sent one of his engineers to clean the lenses. As the engineer walked towards the sensor panel, there was a crankcase explosion that killed him instantly. The ship was disabled at sea for a few hours and later had to be towed to the nearest port. Most engineers know that the immediate reaction to an OMD alarm is to slow down the engine. Overthinking his options and their consequences delayed the chief engineer's decision making. This delay cost a precious life and a few hundred thousand dollars in damage.

In moments where there is confusion, uncertainty, and possibly chaos, the leader has to make quick decisions. He needs clarity of thought to identify the best course of action in limited time.

Over-analysis causes decision paralysis. Neither can you wait too long for perfect information. A Golden Stripes leader has to make decisions with whatever information is available.

I have found using 'heuristic models' or 'mental shortcuts' very effective at sea. At least 80 per cent of all situations at sea are foreseeable and can be dealt with using this method. Complex problems don't always need complex solutions. They can be as simple as 'when you get an OMD alarm, slow down the engine'.

Heuristics help us take instant decisions at stressful times when our brains struggle to cope up with new, unexpected situations. If you remember and follow the heuristic, 'Reduce RPM when the turbochargers surge', your instant actions can prevent an engine breakdown.

Heuristics in navigation are of immense help when decisions have to be made in seconds. Some of these are:

- Never collide without going astern.
- Do not run aground with both the anchors in the pipe.
- When in doubt, slow down.
- In turning basins, keep the speed below 3 knots.

- When making less than 5 knots, there are only two rudder positions – hard-over and amidships.

- Do not go astern in ice.

- An end-on collision is better than a broadside one.

If someone needs CPR (cardiopulmonary resuscitation), apply the heuristic 'CAB': Chest compressions, Airway, Breathing. It can help save a life.

When confronted with a fire, remember 'FIRE': Find, Inform, Restrict, Extinguish.

There are also heuristics or rules of thumb that can help us remember crucial steps even in daily decision making. In the engine room, it could be:

- Ensure adequate generating power is available before starting large electrical motors.

- Blow through before starting and putting generators on load.

- If the remote control fails during manoeuvring, immediately use the local controls. Fault finding can wait.

Leaders can also help their subordinates improve their decision making with specific standing orders and rules of thumb:

- While at sea, keep a minimum distance of 2 nautical miles from ships, and 5 miles off navigation hazards.

- Start altering course at least when the other ship is 5 miles off.

- For every three satellite fixes, use one alternate method of fixing the ship's position.

- It is better to be under way than to anchor in sea-state Beaufort 7 or more.

With the *Green Lily*, simple guidance such as 'Do not berth or unberth in more than 25 knots of wind' could have helped the captain make a quick, safe and effective decision.

(D) DO

Reason and calm judgment, the qualities specially belonging to a leader.

– Tacitus, Roman senator, AD 56

When the pilot took charge of the situation after we lost steering, he was calm.[28] He clearly communicated his orders, with authority and without ambiguity. He got the team together to perform their respective actions, and got the result he wanted.

When checklists, procedures, and heuristics fail, use your instincts to guide your judgments. Instincts are the subconscious processing of all your experience, expertise, past actions, and the current situation. Instinct is your gut feeling. Trust it. Combine this with your fight instinct to find a solution. Take Two to make sure you are not being rash. Then act!

Decide and act with confidence. Do it with calm and composure, even if deep within you're unsure of the outcome. Your confidence will inspire your team to believe that there *is* a solution, and they will be willing to work with you.

(E) EVALUATE EFFECTIVENESS

In a complex system, we should make sure that it is possible to revise any judgment in the wake of failure as soon as it becomes clear that it has flaws.

– Dr Sidney Dekker, *Drift into Failure*

The captain of the *Green Lily* realised that he had made a mistake when he encountered huge waves after sailing out of port. He still had the option of returning back to the safety of the harbour, but chose not to.

Sometimes, we may be afraid of looking silly in correcting a decision we made earlier. There is no shame in making a wrong decision, but it is certainly a discredit if you know that you've made a mistake and don't correct it. The sea will always be mightier than your pride, and will let you know so. Evaluate if you need to reduce speed further or apply more helm. Ask for feedback. Adjust.

Decisiveness is a key characteristic of highly effective leaders. As a Golden Stripes leader, your decisions will take you to the true north of your leadership.

28 Introduction.

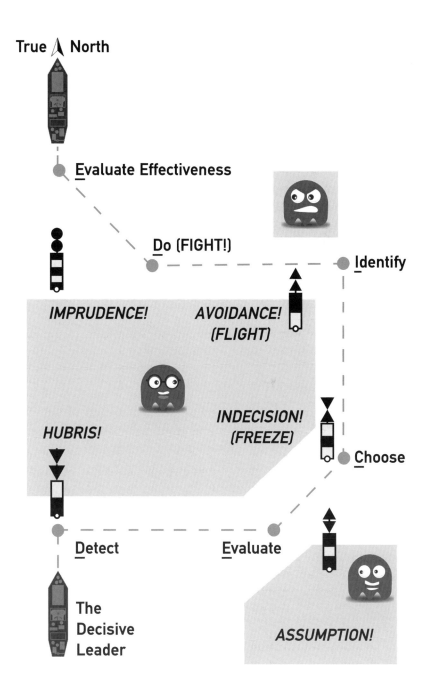

True ⚓ North

Evaluate Effectiveness

Do (FIGHT!)

Identify

IMPRUDENCE!

AVOIDANCE! (FLIGHT)

HUBRIS!

INDECISION! (FREEZE)

Choose

Detect

Evaluate

The Decisive Leader

ASSUMPTION!

The Decision Making Mnemonic ©

DECISIVE LEADERSHIP

- Good judgment is essential for any leader. You get better at it through practice.

- Decisions often have to be made in ambiguous situations, under time pressure. A leader has to balance commercial and safety considerations.

- Beware of the decision traps- (i) Hubris (ii) Assumption, (iii) Indecision, (iv) Avoidance, and (v) Imprudence.

- Subdue the subconscious freeze and flight responses when making a decision; instead consciously tap into your fight response.

- Start with small decisions, and get into the habit.

- Use the DECIDE template; Detect, Evaluate, Choose, Identify, Do, and Evaluate effectiveness.

- Consult with your team so you can carefully evaluate your options.

- A complex problem does not always need a complex solution.

21

EPILOGUE: THE VOYAGE OF LEADERSHIP

Before enlightenment, bring ship into port, overhaul engine

After enlightenment, bring ship into port, overhaul engine!

– Ancient Zen saying (adaption)

ONE OF MY FIRST BIG tests as a ship captain came without warning.

I was on a 690-foot-long container ship, approaching the beautiful Atlantic entrance to the Panama Canal. As is customary, we tested the engines and steering machinery well outside the entrance. We were to transit the canal the next day, and we also had to bunker fuel for the rest of the voyage. The Marine Traffic Control enquired over the radio whether I was comfortable anchoring the ship inside the breakwater without pilot assistance. I knew I was, and I said so. Having picked out a spot to anchor, we began our manoeuvre to bring the ship inside the crowded anchorage.

There are treacherous currents that flow across the entrance of the Cristobal harbour. Ships counter the effect of these currents by keeping a robust speed while entering the narrow opening of the breakwater. So we entered at a speed of about 5 knots. We planned to go astern on the engines as soon as we entered the harbour, and then manoeuvre gently into the anchorage. But I was soon to learn that plans are plans, and an engine is only as good as its last kick.

There was a big 'whoosh' from down below just as the bow entered inside the breakwater. The chief engineer called to report that one of the engine liner gaskets had burst. If we continued operating the engines, we risked damaging the liner surface. And we would be unable to transit the canal the next morning, meaning the precious cold cargo would have to sit in its boxes for longer. I assured the chief engineer I would not use the engines if I could help it. At the same time, I was also aware that I would be compelled to use the engines if required for the safety of the ship, which was more important than meeting the schedule. Thankfully, we found a solution that was both safe and didn't affect the ship's schedule.

When I had assumed command of the vessel months before, one of the first things I did was familiarise myself with the ship. I assessed its behaviour including minimum steerage speed and residual momentum from various speeds. I also studied how the ship would react to different wind conditions, taking into account many scenarios. Eventually, I was so familiar with the ship that it had become an extension of me. I stored this information in both my conscious and my subconscious. And that day, when the engines failed after entering the breakwater, all of this came back in a flash to help me in my hour of need.

My ship was still half a nautical mile away from the anchoring position, and I quickly calculated that it could travel (just about) this distance with its current momentum. Feeling reassured by this knowledge, I calmly turned the ship into the gap between two other anchored ships. Meanwhile, I instructed my officer on watch to alert the Marine Traffic Control of our situation and request tug assistance.

It was a congested anchorage with plenty of ships waiting for their transit. All the ship-handling skills I had honed over the years and all the tricks I had learnt from my seniors came into play. I deftly manoeuvred my ship between the other ships and swung it in just the right direction before dropping the anchor. The best part was that we were able to anchor at the precise spot where we had earlier planned before the engine failure. The crew cheered. We made it safely into the anchorage. (Good thing too, else we would have ended up on the evening news!)

Many things could have gone wrong on that day. The chief engineer could have delayed informing me of the situation; our anchors could have been poorly maintained, not deploying when we needed them to; I could have panicked and frozen, or worse, swerved and hit an oncoming ship; I could have used the engine and damaged it enough to delay the Panama transit; my team could have been ill-prepared for an emergency, creating chaos and making mistakes in the execution of our response.

Instead, the entire team on the ship worked as one efficient unit. The Marine Traffic Control conveyed their relief that the incident hadn't escalated into a serious situation; a good thing, as it turned out that the port didn't have a tugboat which could have assisted us in time.

All my team members were unique personalities and came from different cultural and social backgrounds. These differences could have manifested themselves on that day by way of communication errors, confusion, and an accident. But everyone played their role perfectly. The chief engineer prepared for an emergency manoeuvre, and one of my officers gave me continuous situation reports, while another prepared the anchors. Despite our differences, we had used the various teamwork tools and adopted the right mindsets to build ourselves into a cohesive team. Our differences did not matter; what mattered was that together we made a difference!

Knowing my ship well and having prepared for such a situation helped me act effectively. Our calm approach and decisive action helped us achieve what every mariner sets out to do: get his ship safely into and out of port. That day, I saw our golden stripes shining brighter than usual.

AN ACTION PLAN FOR SUCCESS: FULL AHEAD

The potential of the average person is like a huge ocean unsailed, a new continent unexplored, a world of possibilities waiting to be released and channelled toward some great good.

– Brian Tracy, entrepreneur

I learnt a great deal during my many years at sea; from the day I stood on the bridge as a shaken-up third officer, confused after a steering loss, to the day I took control of a similar situation as captain, bringing my ship to safety. I have shared these lessons in leadership with you in this book. I hope you will have gained some insights that you'll apply and use to succeed, while avoiding the mistakes I made.

As you build your action plan for success, remember this: make small changes one at a time to build positive habits; reflect on stories with powerful lessons, and calibrate your mindset.

Lastly, you don't need anyone's permission to become the leader you want to be. Each of us has enormous potential within us to be a great leader. You don't have to accept your life as it is; go full ahead and *lead* your life. You alone have the power and the responsibility to make improvements in all areas of your work. Expect more from yourself than what others expect from you. Why? Simply because you owe yourself a great career. So keep at it and be consistent. Make every day a masterpiece in leadership.

We all need milestones, or waypoints, to tell us how our voyage of leadership is going. So, how will you know you're on the path to better leadership? The answer is simple: If you are making things better, you're being a good leader. Also,

- you will observe a better safety and operational record on your ship.
- work will get done faster.
- your crew will work well with you and with each other.
- you will find yourself making better decisions and getting better results.

You will also find yourself enjoying your career more than before. Despite all the challenges around you, you will feel better – professionally, physically, and spiritually.

Leadership is the most important quality of a Golden Stripes mariner. Your colleagues, your family, the industry, and the planet all need your unique leadership abilities to change the world for the better. The only way to get there is with your daily commitment to improve and practise everything that I've shared with you.

Start today. Today is the first day of the rest of your life, and your best is yet to come.

Remember, your leadership is both the journey and the destination. Let your stripes shine bright. *Bon Voyage!*

ABOUT THE AUTHOR: CAPTAIN VS PARANI

Seawater runs in Parani's veins. He was only 18 months old when he sat on the captain's chair on the bridge of a passenger ship. (Actually, he was sitting on the captain's lap, after slipping away from his parents.)

Who knew that only 28 years later, he would be sitting on the captain's chair again … but this time, as a real captain, one the youngest in the shipping company MSC's fleet history.

When he grew up on the Andaman Islands in the Bay of Bengal, everything revolved around the sea, from how to spend the weekend to when the stores would be restocked from the supply ships.

His parents knew he loved the sea, but they were surprised when, unlike them, he eschewed going to college, and chose instead to enlist as a ship's cadet at 17. For 12 years, he steadily worked his way up through the ranks, starting as a deckhand and eventually becoming second-in-command. During his vacations, he would take on extra assignments: assisting a mooring master to berth oil tankers, training at nautical schools, and even working as a marine advisor to a shipping company. At the age of 29, he landed his own command.

Parani did eventually go back to college (much to the relief of his father, a banker for nearly four decades), earning master's degrees in business law (LLM) and business administration (MBA), then rounded his education out with a practitioner's certificate in neurolinguistic programming (NLP).

After sitting for an exam for the Institute of Chartered Shipbrokers and achieving first spot worldwide, Parani flew to London for the awards. This recognition caught the eye of his shipping company, who were quick to offer him a job in Hong Kong, to head their safety and quality department. After seven years, the company asked Parani to head their crewing and training department in Cyprus, where he is responsible for over 8,000 seafarers who operate 185 vessels worldwide.

Switching from seafaring captain to corporate executive gave Parani the chance to start a family. He married an architect from his native India and they welcomed their first child into the world in 2007. In recognition of his efforts, his company recently named a ship *MSC Uma*, after his daughter.

Parani currently lives in Limassol, Cyprus, with his wife and daughter, and their two cats.

While Parani still longs for the open sea, he loves being a senior executive in a multinational shipping company. His unique background and experience let him provide fresh insights into ship- and shore-based operations, allowing him to influence literally thousands of seafarers and executives alike.

SALUTES: DEDICATIONS

THIS BOOK IS DEDICATED to the brave men and women at sea, past and present. Far away from the warmth of their homes, they have found continents and moved people and cargo across the seas.

Shipping is not possible without its leaders ashore. The ship owners and managers, financiers, insurers, pilots, unions, trainers, journalists, and maritime organisations all contribute to the pool of maritime knowledge. The spiritual leaders at the Mission to Seafarers provide comfort to all mariners. In recognition of their selfless efforts, part of the proceeds from this book will help put a copy into every location where the Mission works.

A special dedication to the families of the mariners, who steady the boat at home while their spouses are at sea. My wife Vidhya is my ever supportive 'first mate'. She is also the first editor of this book. My daughter Uma has been my happiness officer. My parents are the shipyard where I was built and they have always offered me unconditional love; they are the first leaders that I knew. My brother Vijay has been my safety officer, being the voice of reason, whether or not I needed one!

Captain Leveyl Gomez supported the concept of this book, and along the way gave me his brutally honest reviews. He has been my friend since childhood; he is my shipmate for life. Another old friend of mine, Vamsi Krishna, vetted the engineering case studies and provided valuable feedback.

Like in shipping, the publishing of the book has been a fantastic international collaboration. I've been fortunate to have a great team rowing with me. Demetris Stylianides of Thinkbox Ltd, Cyprus; Derek Lewis of Derek Lewis Ink, Louisiana, USA; Vijay Ghosh and Avantica David of the9Words, India; Dr Keith Whittles and Sue Steven of Whittles Publishing, Scotland – all helped me complete my voyage with this book.

I am also grateful to everyone who helped shape my leadership skills, including my colleagues at the Mediterranean Shipping

Company (MSC), and fellow professionals at The Nautical Institute (NI), The Institute of Chartered Shipbokers (ICS), and the Institute of Marine Engineering, Science & Technology (IMarEST).

I would like to add that the views represented in this book, including any errors or omissions, are solely my own.

I thank you, the reader, for choosing to read this book, and I look forward to hearing from you. You can get in touch with me and share your feedback through my website: www.parani.org.

Captain VS Parani

Limassol

GOLDEN STRIPES RESOURCES

A man builds on the expertise and knowledge of those before him. This book would not have been possible without the knowledge that I have gained over the years from various people, many of whom I have never met but only read their works.

In order to ensure that *Golden Stripes* would become an invaluable resource for leadership on the high seas, I consulted the following to help develop my understanding on the subject.

Abrashoff, Captain Michael D, *It's Your Ship*, ISBN: 978-1-4555-2302-3.

Adair, John, *Effective Communication: The Most Important Management Skill of All*, ASIN: B00FFBQPCG.

Anderton, BH (2002), 'Ageing of the brain', *Mechanisms of Ageing and Development*, 123(7): 811-817.

Appelo, Jurgen, *Managing for Happiness: Games, Tools, and Practices to Motivate Any Team*, ISBN: 978-1-1192-6868-0.

Bandura, Albert, *Social Foundations of Thought and Action: A Social Cognitive Theory*, ISBN: 858-0000940367.

Baron, Neil, *Power Poses: Tweaking Your Body Language for Greater Success*. Expert Perspective, Fast Company.

Bereiter, Carl, and Marlene Scardamalia, *Surpassing Ourselves*, ISBN: 978-0-8126-9204-4.

Cialdini, Robert B *Influence, The Psychology of Persuasion*, ISBN: 978-0-06-124189-5.

Cialdini, Robert B, Nick Morgan, and Deborah Tannen (*Harvard Business Review* staff) *HBR'S 10 Must Reads – On Communication*, ISBN: 978-1-4221-8986-3.

Cohen, William A (PhD), *Drucker on Leadership*, ISBN: 978-0-470-40500-0.

Colcombe, SJ, KI Erickson, PE Scalf, JS Kim, R Prakash, E McAuley, S Elavsky, DX Marquez, L Hu, and AF Kramer, (2006), 'Aerobic exercise training increases brain volume in aging humans'. *Journal of Gerontology*, 61A(11): 1166–1170.

Cornah, D *(2006),* 'The impact of spirituality on mental health: a review of the literature', *Mental Health Foundation*, ISBN: 978-1-903645-85-7.

Cuddy, Amy JC, Susan T Fiske, Peter Glick and Jun Xu, (2002), 'A model of (often mixed) stereotype content: Competence and warmth respectively follow from perceived status and competition', *Journal of Personality and Social Psychology*, 82-(6): 878–902.

Deal, TE, and AA Kennedy, *Corporate Cultures: The Rites and Rituals of Corporate Life,* ISBN: 978-0-7382-0330-0.

Dekker, Sidney, *Drift into Failure: From Hunting Broken Components to Understanding Complex Systems,* ISBN: 978-1-4094-2221-1.

Dillon, Karen, *HBR Guide to Office Politics,* ASIN: B00O92Q6EE.

Drucker, Peter F, *Managing Oneself,* ISBN: 978-1-4221-2312-6.

Dweck, Carol, *Mind-set: How You Can Fulfill Your Potential,* ASIN: B00ZLW6OK2.

Ericsson, K Anders, and Jacqui Smith, *Towards a General Theory of Expertise: Prospects and Limits,* ISBN: 978-0-5214-0612-3.

Ericsson, K Anders and Robert Pool, *Peak: Secrets from the New Science of Expertise,* ASIN: B019CH3M10.

Ericsson, K Anders, Neil Charness, Paul J Feltovich, and Robert R Hoffman, *The Cambridge Handbook of Expertise and Expert Performance,* ISBN: 978-0-5216-0081-1.

Fatigue at Sea, www.project-horizon.eu.

Gigerenzer, G, and W Gaissmaier, (2011), 'Heuristic decision making', *Annual Review of Psychology,* 62: 451-482.

Gregory, Dik, and Paul Shanahan, *The Human Element: A Guide to Human Behaviour in the Shipping Industry,* ISBN: 978-0-1155-3120-0.

Gruenert, Steve, and Todd Whitaker, *School Culture Rewired: How to Define, Assess, and Transform It,* ISBN: 978-1-4166-1990-1.

Hafey, Robert B, *Lean Safety: Transforming your Safety Culture with Lean Management,* ISBN: 978-1-4398-1642-4.

Halliwell, Ed, Liz Main and Celia Richardson (2000), *The Fundamental Facts,* Mental Health Foundation, ISBN: 978-1-903645-93-2.

Harle, PG (1994) 'Investigation of human factors: The link to accident prevention.' In N Johnston, N McDonald, and R Fuller (eds), *Aviation Psychology in Practice.*

Harvard Healthy Eating Plate, The, http://www.health.harvard.edu/healthy-eating-plate.

Horne, J and LA Reyner, (1995) 'Sleep-related vehicle accidents', *British Medical Journal,* 310: 565–567.

Isaac, AR (1992), 'Mental Practice – Does It Work in the Field?' *The Sport Psychologist,* 6: 192-198.

Kahneman, Daniel, *Thinking, Fast and Slow,* ISBN: 978-0-1410-3357-0.

Klein, Gary, *The Power of Intuition: How to Use Your Gut Feelings to Make Better Decisions,* ISBN: 978-0-3855-0289-4.

Koch, Richard, *The 80/20 Principle: The Secret to Achieving More with Less,* ISBN: 978-0-3854-9174-7.

Kouzes, James M and Barry Z Posner, *The Leadership Challenge,* ISBN: 978-0-4706-5172-8.

Landy, Frank J and Jeffrey M Conte, *Work in the 21st Century: An Introduction to Industrial and Organizational Psychology,* ISBN: 978-1-118-29120-7.

Levy, Paul E , *Industrial Organizational Psychology: Understanding the Workplace,* ISBN: 978-0618526406.

Luft, Joseph (1961), 'The Johari Window, a graphic model of interpersonal awareness', *Human Relations Training News,* 5(1), 6-7.

Marquet, L David, *Turn the Ship Around! A True Story of Turning Followers into Leaders,* ISBN: 978-1-5918-4640-6.

Martin, KA, and CR Hall, (1995), 'Using Mental Imagery to Enhance Intrinsic Motivation', *Journal of Sport and Exercise Psychology,* 17(1): 54-69.

Mayo, Andrew, *The Human Value of the Enterprise*: *Valuing People as Assets-Monitoring, Measuring, Managing,* ISBN: 978-1-8578-8281-0.

Mental Health Foundation (2002), 'Out at work', 3(16).

Mol, Tania, *Productive Safety Management,* ISBN: 978-0-7506-5922-2.

Murphy, John J, *Pulling Together: The Power of Teamwork,* ISBN: 978-1-6081-0072-9.

Nautical Institute, *The Nautical Institute on Command,* ISBN: 978-1-9069-1521-6.

NHS: http://www.nhs.uk/conditions/stress-anxiety-depression/pages/benefits-of-talking-therapy.aspx.

Nutt, Paul C, *Why Decisions Fail,* ASIN: B015QL5XKE.

Reason, James (1997), *Managing the Risks of Organizational Accidents,* ASIN: B01B14Q9RE.

Roughton, James, *Safety Culture: An Innovative Leadership Approach,* ISBN: 978-0-1239-6496-0.

Safe Work Australia, *How to Manage Work Health and Safety Issues, Code of Practice,* ISBN: 978-0-6423-3301-8.

Schein, Edgar H, *Organizational Culture and Leadership,* ISBN: 978-0-4701-9060-9.

Seppälä, Emma, and Kim Cameron, ''Proof That Positive Work Cultures Are More Productive', *Harvard Business Review,* https://hbr.org/2015/12/proof-that-positive-work-cultures-are-more-productive.

Shackleton, Ernest, *South: The* Endurance *Expedition,* ISBN: 978-0-4511-9880-8.

Shallenberger, Steven R, *Becoming Your Best, The 12 Principles of Highly Successful Leaders*, ISBN: 978-0-0718-3998-3.

St George, Andrew, *Royal Navy Way of Leadership*, ISBN: 978-1 8480-9344- 7.

Sternberg, Robert J, *Psychology of Abilities, Competencies and Expertise* (*Chapter 9: Biological Intelligence*), ISBN: 0521007763.

Taylor, CB , JF Sallis and R Needle (1985), 'The relation of physical activity and exercise to mental health', *Public Health Reports,* 100(2): 195–202, PMCID: PMC1424736.

US Department of Transportation, Federal Aviation Administration, Advisory Circular 60-22, *Aeronautical Decision-Making.*

Weeks, Holly, *Failure to Communicate,* ISBN: 978-1-4221-3749-9.

West, Michael A, *Effective Teamwork: Practical Lessons from Organizational Research,* ISBN: 978-0-4709-7497-1.

Wethey, David, *Decide: Better Ways of making Better Decisions,* ASIN: B00AZJZ5O2.

Wiersma, Bill, *The Power of Professionalism – The Seven Mind-Sets That Drive Performance and Build Trust,* ISBN: 978-1-9328-8104-2.

Williams, Melvin G Sr, and Melvin G Williams Jr, *Navigating the Seven Seas,* ISBN: 978-1-59114-960-6.

Williamson, AM, and Anne-Marie Feyer, (1995), 'Moderate sleep deprivation produces impairments in cognitive and motor performance equivalent to legally prescribed levels of alcohol intoxication', *Occupational and Environmental Medicine*, 57: 649–655.

Wray, Rear Admiral Robert O Jr, USN, *Saltwater Leadership,* ISBN: 978-1-61251-212-9.

Young, KW (2012), 'Positive effects of spirituality on quality of life for people with severe mental illness', *International Journal of Psychosocial Rehabilitation,* 16(2): 62-77.

Young, Michael and Johan Muller, *Knowledge, Expertise and the Professions,* ISBN: 978-0-4157-1391-7.

Zieve, David (MD, MHA) and David R Eltz, *Stress Management*, US National Library of Medicine, http://www.nlm.nih.gov/medlineplus/ency/article/001942.htm.

Investigation Reports

Australian Transport Safety Bureau Marine Occurrence Investigation, *ID Integrity*, 294-MO-2012-005.

Australian Transport Safety Bureau, ATSB Transport Safety Report, Marine Occurrence Investigation No. 257MO-2008-009 involving the bulk carrier *Great Majesty*.

British Wreck Commissioner's report, *Titanic* Disaster, 1912, investigation report, Washington Printing Office.

8074, Formal investigation into the sinking of the *Herald of Free Enterprise*, ISBN: 0-11-550828-7.

Det Norske Veritas (DNV), casualty information, No.5 of 2007.

Det Norske Veritas (DNV), Managing Risk, Engine room fires can be avoided, 2000. Further guidance is also available on the IMO, Maritime Safety Committee (MSC)/Circular 647 (adopted 6 June 1994), Guidelines to minimise leakages from flammable liquid systems.

Federal Bureau of Maritime Casualty Investigation (BSU), Germany, Investigation Report 301/09, Occupational Accident on board the *TMV ECE Nur K* on the Lower Elbe on 1 August 2009.

Federal Bureau of Maritime Casualty Investigation (BSU), Germany, Investigation report 329/03, Fatal Casualty in the Scavenge Air Receiver of the Main Engine of the *CMS London Express*.

Gard, A crew claims statistical analysis, 1993–2004.

Hong Kong Special Administrative Region, Marine Department, Marine Accident Investigation Section, Report of investigation into the death of the relieving chief engineer on the Hong Kong registered bulk carrier *Apollo* in Hong Kong on 24 August 2011.

International Group of P&I Clubs, Pilotage sub-committee report on pilot error related claims over US$100,000 from 20.02.99 to 20.02.04.

Lloyd's Law Reports, Papera Traders Co. Ltd and Others vs Hyundai Merchant Marine Co. Ltd and Others ('The Eurasian Dream'), [2002] EWHC 118 (Comm).

Marine Accident Investigation Branch Safety Digest 1/2005, Case 3, Fatal accident to a Chief Officer of a dry cargo ship. Also, see IMO, Lessons learned for presentation to seafarers (FSI 20, Case 7).

Marine Accident Investigation Branch, UK, Accident Investigation Report, *Braer*. Reproduced under the Click-Use Licence of the UK Office of Public Sector Information (OPSI).

Marine Accident Investigation Branch, UK, Report 5/99, *Green Lily*. Reproduced under the Click-Use Licence of the UK Office of Public Sector Information (OPSI).

Marine Accident Investigation Branch, UK, Report No. 16/2004. Death of the 40-year-old Russian deckhand, Sergey Gaponov on the ship *Sea Melody*.

Marine Accident Investigation Branch, Review of lifeboats and launching systems accidents, Safety Study 1/2001.

Marine Accident Investigation Branch, UK, Listing, flooding and grounding of vehicle carrier *Hoegh Osaka*. Report 6-2016. Reproduced under the Click-Use Licence of the UK Office of Public Sector Information (OPSI).

Marine Accident Investigation Branch UK, Report No 02/10, Report on the investigation of the grounding of MV *Maersk Kendal* on Monggok Sebarok reef in the Singapore Strait on 16 September 2009.

National Transportation Safety Board of the United States of America, Marine Accident Report, Report No. NTSB/MAR-90/04. Grounding of the U.S. tankship Exxon Valdez on Bligh Reef, Prince William Sound, Near Valdez, Alaska, March 24, 1989.

NTSB/MAR-09/02, Allision of Bahamas-Registered Tankship M/T *Axel Spirit* with Ambrose Light Entrance to New York Harbor, November 3, 2007.

National Transportation Safety Board PB97-916401, grounding of the *Royal Majesty* on Rose and Crown Shoal near Nantucket, Massachusetts.

Transport Accident Investigation Commission (TAIC), New Zealand, Inquiry 10-204, Bulk carrier *Hanjin Bombay*, grounding, Mount Maunganui, 21 June 2010.

United States Coast Guard, Report on the explosion and the sinking of the chemical tanker *Bow Mariner* in the Atlantic Ocean on 28 February 2004.

US District Court for the District of Maryland: *USA vs Grifakis*, Case No. 1:11-cr-00011.

USEFUL LINKS: A SEA OF KNOWLEDGE

- **Personality Assessment Tests (Your Self-Image)**
  - http://www.humanmetrics.com
  - http://personality-testing.info
- **Shipping Industry News**
  - http://www.imo.org/KnowledgeCentre/ CurrentAwarenessBulletin
- **Accident Reports (Learning from the Mistakes of Others)**
  - http://www.nautinst.org/en/forums/mars
  - https://www.chirp.co.uk
  - https://www.gov.uk/government/organisations/marine-accident-investigation-branch
  - http://www.bsu-bund.de/EN/Home/homepage_node.html
  - http://www.ntsb.gov/investigations/AccidentReports
- **Health and Nutrition (You Can Be What You Want To Be)**
  - http://www.hsph.harvard.edu/nutritionsource
  - http://www.mayoclinic.org/healthy-lifestyle
  - http://www.nhs.uk/livewell/fitness/Pages/Fitnesshome.aspx
  - http://www.nlm.nih.gov/medlineplus/ exerciseandphysicalfitness.html

- **Professional Associations (Good Company)**
  - Nautical Institute, http://www.nautinst.org
  - Institute of Marine Engineers, http://www.imarest.org
- **Loss-Prevention Information (Prevention Is Better Than Cure)**
  - http://www.ukpandi.com
  - http://www.nepia.com
  - http://www.standard-club.com
  - http://www.gard.no
  - http://www.skuld.com
  - http://www.swedishclub.com
- **International Maritime Organization**
  - www.imo.org
- **Maritime Security**
  - https://icc-ccs.org/piracy-reporting-centre/live-piracy-map
- **Port State Control and Government Circulars**
  - AMSA, Australia https://www.amsa.gov.au
  - MCA UK, https://www.gov.uk/government/organisations/maritime-and-coastguard-agency
  - US Coast Guard, https://homeport.uscg.mil
- **Author Website**:
  - www.parani.org

Visit the author's website to connect with the author, access further useful links, and leave feedback.

Pictorial Index of Golden Stripes: Leader-Ship on the High Seas

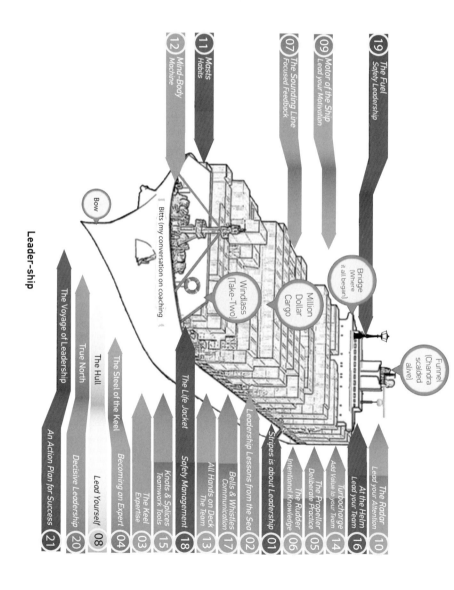

Leader-ship

19 The Fuel
Safety Leadership

09 Motor of the Ship
Lead your Motivation

07 The Sounding Line
Focused Feedback

11 Masts
Habits

12 Mind-Body
Machine

Bow

Bitts (my conversation on coaching

Bridge
(Where
it all began)

Funnel
(Chandra
scalded
alive)

Windlass
(Take-Two)

Million
Dollar
Cargo

The Voyage of Leadership

True North

The Hull

The Steel of the Keel

The Life Jacket

Leadership Lessons from the Sea

Stripes is about Leadership

An Action Plan for Success 21

Decisive Leadership 20

Lead Yourself 08

Becoming an Expert 04

The Keel
Expertise 03

Knots & Splices
Teamwork Tools 15

Safety Management 18

All Hands on Deck
The Team 13

Bells & Whistles
Communication 17

Stripes is about Leadership 01

Leadership Lessons from the Sea 02

Intentional Knowledge 06

The Propeller
Deliberate Practice 05

Turbocharge
Add Value to your Team 14

At the Helm
Lead your Team 16

The Radar
Lead your Attention 10